WORKING WITH CHILDREN FROM CULTURALLY DIVERSE BACKGROUNDS

D0145758

WORKING WITH CHILDREN FROM CULTURALLY DIVERSE BACKGROUNDS

M. Diane Klein, Ph.D.
California State University, Los Angeles
and
Deborah Chen, Ph.D.
California State University, Northridge

DELMAR
CENGAGE Learning™

Australia • Brazil • Japan • Korea • Mexico • Singapore • Spain • United Kingdom • United States

Working with Children From Culturally Diverse Backgrounds
M. Diane Klein, Deborah Chen

Business Unit Director: Susan L. Simpfenderfer

Acquisitions Editor: Erin O'Connor Traylor

Editorial Assistant: Alexis Ferraro

Executive Marketing Manager: Donna J. Lewis

Channel Manager: Nigar Hale

Executive Production Manager: Wendy A. Troeger

Production Editor: J.P. Henkel

Cover Design: Judi Orozco

For product information and technology assistance, contact us at **Cengage Learning Customer & Sales Support, 1-800-354-9706**

For permission to use material from this text or product, submit all requests online at **www.cengage.com/permissions**
Further permissions questions can be emailed to **permissionrequest@cengage.com**

Library of Congress Control Number: 00-034646

ISBN-13: 978-0-7668-2406-5

ISBN-10: 0-7668-2406-3

Delmar
Executive Woods
5 Maxwell Drive
Clifton Park, NY 12065
USA

Cengage Learning is a leading provider of customized learning solutions with office locations around the globe, including Singapore, the United Kingdom, Australia, Mexico, Brazil, and Japan. Locate your local office at **international.cengage.com/region**

Cengage Learning products are represented in Canada by Nelson Education, Ltd.

For your lifelong learning solutions, visit **www.cengage.com/delmar**

Visit our corporate website at **www.cengage.com**

Printed in the United States of America
4 5 6 7 8   15 14 13 12 11

FD175

Dedication

To Bill and Mary Alexander
who taught me to value the "diversity" in all of us,
and to Micah, Nancy, Crystal, Carlos, Sarah,
Erin, and all the children
who have helped me love and appreciate
their differences and their uniqueness.

— MDK

Special recognition to my parents,
Winnie and Philip Chen,
for my Chinese-Jamaican heritage
and for my introduction to cultural diversity.

— DC

CONTENTS

PREFACE

In light of the changing demographics of the United States, the purpose of this book is to present an overview of the ways in which cultural differences can influence young children's behavior, communication, and learning styles. It also intends to assist early childhood professionals in the critical task of examining their own values, practices, and biases, and in understanding how their own culture influences their professional attitudes and practices. It is intended as a practical guide for early childhood staff working in such settings as group childcare, preschools, and Head Start programs. We have attempted to provide both a simple framework for understanding cultural variability, as well as hands-on suggestions for teachers and staff working with infants and preschool age children in multicultural, multiethnic, and multilingual environments.

The book is not intended to be an exhaustive text on this vast and complex topic. Nor is the book intended to be a descriptive inventory of various ethnic and racial groups. The descriptions and examples of specific cultures included in the book are intended only to be suggestive of the kinds of differences that *may* exist across groups. The book intends to increase the early childhood practitioner's understanding of the ways culture can influence family values and child-rearing practices, as well as children's behaviors and perceptions.

The book begins with two chapters that provide a brief overview of the various aspects of "culture" and its potential implications for early childhood programs. The third chapter takes a fairly detailed look at how child-rearing practices and values may be influenced by culture. It presents an overview of the range of variability in child-rearing practices across cultures, and ways in which this may impact families' expectations and interactions with early childhood programs.

Subsequent chapters focus on children rather than families. These chapters consider the curriculum content areas of language and communication (including both communication styles and learning English as a second language), social skills and behavior (including the development of bias and prejudice), and school readiness and emergent literacy. These chapters attempt to give the reader an understanding of how culture can influence young children's development and behavior in these areas. In addition, these chapters provide examples of curriculum and instructional adaptations that can be used to accommodate children from diverse backgrounds.

The final chapter contains a brief discussion of professional development and multicultural competencies in the field of early childhood education. Although the book is written at the introductory level, its contents are intended to include readily understandable and useable information which can be easily translated into daily early childhood practice

M. Diane Klein, Ph.D.
Deborah Chen, Ph.D.

Acknowledgments

The authors wish to express their appreciation to Dr. Phil Chinn for his contributions and conversations about multicultural education, to the reviewers for their helpful suggestions for improving the manuscript, and to Delmar for publishing this book. We particularly want to thank the families, children, and staff at Centro de Ninos, whose dedication to children's joyful learning so inspired the pages of this book, and to the many other families from diverse backgrounds who have shared their homes, stories, and lives, and have guided our crosscultural journey. Special thanks is given to Anne Marie Richardson-Gibbs for taking the wonderful Central de Ninos photos that appear throughout the book.

About the Authors

M. Diane Klein, Ph.D., Professor
Division of Special Education, Charter College of Education,
California State University, Los Angeles

Dr. M. Diane Klein is a professor of early childhood special education in the Division of Special Education at California State University, Los Angeles, where she coordinates the credential, M.A., and certificate programs in Early Childhood Special Education. These programs emphasize the training of early intervention personnel to work in urban multicultural environments. Dr. Klein has a background in speech pathology and audiology, and developmental psychology. She has directed numerous federal grant projects related to inclusion support skills and methods in early childhood special education, and has developed early intervention programs and training materials which serve high-risk families from multicultural backgrounds. Her recent publications have focused on curriculum development and strategies for inclusion of children with disabilities in early childhood settings, and caregiver/child interaction with infants and young children with multiple disabilities. Dr. Klein frequently conducts in-service training in the area of development of communication skills in young children, curriculum development in early childhood special education, and inclusion support strategies. She also serves on numerous boards and committees related to early intervention services in the state of California, and is the Executive Director of Centro de Ninos y Padres Early Intervention Program which serves culturally diverse families in the East Los Angeles area.

Deborah Chen, Ph.D., Professor
Department of Special Education, College of Education
California State University, Northridge

Deborah Chen, Ph.D., is a professor in the College of Education at California State University, Northridge, where she teaches in the master's and credential programs in Early Childhood Special Education. Her extensive background in working with families and young children as a service provider, program administrator, and in-service instructor includes the administration of several federally funded projects related to professional development in early intervention, early childhood special education, and working with families of diverse cultural and linguistic backgrounds. Her research and publications have focused on early communication in infants with multiple disabilities and effective practices for working with families from diverse cultures. Dr. Chen has provided leadership in developing in-service training models and materials in these area of professional development in California and other states. She has been invited to conduct courses throughout the United States, Australia, Canada, the Netherlands, Taiwan, and Thailand.

WORKING WITH CHILDREN FROM CULTURALLY DIVERSE BACKGROUNDS

❖ CHAPTER 1

Cultural Diversity in Our Contemporary Society

Jennifer Gregg is a new preschool teacher in an early child-hood program in a large urban area of southern California. Last May, she completed her major in Child Development at a local college in the central valley area where she was born and raised. This is Jennifer's first experience living in a big city, and her first job as a preschool teacher. As Jennifer looks at the children playing in her room, she is struck by the diversity of the group. Some of the children have names she does not know how to pronounce; others are familiar. Names such as: Anise Ahamed, Letricia Bab-cock, Maxine Clark, Amy Dubois, Meiyung Dung, Carrie Harmon, Don Hanson, Lisa Jacobs, Tommy Jones, Carlos Lopez, Mei-Mei Kwan, Matthew Klein, Joaquin Martinez, Paquita Morales, Tracy Nakashima, Leroy Smith, Philip Takeshita, Henry Woo, Scott Wilson, and Nora Zvi. Jennifer has been assigned a bilingual teaching assistant because two of the children are from Spanish-speaking homes. Jennifer's supervisor also told her that she may be able to recruit a student intern in Child Development who speaks Vietnamese because one student speaks very little English. Jennifer is nervous about her responsibility to pro-vide a meaningful learning experience for these preschool-ers. And she wonders how she will get to know each family.

Recent national statistics (Knight, 1997) emphasize the rich cultural, linguistic, and ethnic diversity of this country. The immigrant population of the United States is at its highest level since the 1930s. One out of every 10 people in the United States were born in an-other country. In the 1950s, three-quarters of the im-migrant population were from Europe or Canada. In contrast, the largest number of today's newcomers are from Mexico (27 percent), from other parts of Central and South America (12 percent), and from Asia (27 per-cent). We all experience the diversity of our society through the media, in everyday interactions with peo-ple in our communities, and when working with chil-dren and families in preschool settings.

Special thanks to Dr. Philip Chinn for his time and expertise in coauthoring this chapter.

❖ PURPOSE OF THIS BOOK

In light of the changing demographics of the United States, the purpose of this book is to present an overview of the ways in which cultural differences can influence young children's behavior, communication, and learning styles. It is intended as a practical guide for early childhood staff working in settings such as group day care, preschools, and Head Start programs. The authors of this book have provided a framework within which to view cultural variability and hands-on suggestions for teachers and staff working with infants and preschool age children in multicultural, multiethnic, and multilingual environments. The book is not intended to be an exhaustive text on this vast and complex topic, nor is it intended to be a descriptive inventory of various ethnic and racial groups. The descriptions and examples of specific cultures included here are intended only to be suggestive of the kinds of differences which may exist across groups. It is important that these examples *not* contribute to the development of stereotypes.

❖ OVERVIEW

This chapter, Cultural Diversity in our Contemporary Society, presents a basic framework and the terminology necessary for considering and understanding the various aspects of culture and their implications in early childhood programs. The book is intended to be simple and basic. Those readers who need a more thorough presentation of this topic are referred to sources such as Gollnick & Chinn (1994) and Lynch & Hanson (1998). The next chapter, Creating Culturally Responsive Early Childhood Environments, directs the reader in examining the implications of culture within the context of the early childhood program, and presents a framework by which the reader can examine and/or develop professional practices. Chapter 3, Understanding Cultural Differences in Family Child-Rearing Practices, presents an overview of the range of variability in child-rearing practices across cultures, and ways in which this may impact families' expectations and interactions with early childhood programs. Subsequent chapters address the issues and adaptations related to the developmental domains of language and communication, social skills, school readiness, and emergent literacy more specifically.

❖ THE DIMENSIONS OF CULTURE

Anthropologists define culture as a way of perceiving, believing, evaluating, and behaving (Goodenough, 1987). A common culture provides shared views of the world, values and beliefs, roles and relationships, and patterns of behavior. Characteristics of a culture are based on a shared heritage derived from race, ethnicity, nationality, and other dimensions of diversity. Culture is a blueprint that determines how each of us thinks, feels, perceives, and ultimately behaves. Our values, nonverbal communication, and language are all evidence of our culture. Our cultural identities are influenced by the different subgroups to which we each belong (ethnicity, age, gender, religion, language, socioeconomic class, geographic location) and the emphasis we place on our membership in the subgroups (Gollnick & Chinn, 1994). The way that children in your class respond to you as an adult and a teacher is determined by their families' culture. How they dress, speak, think, and behave are all culture related. What their families have for dinner is determined by culture, ethnicity, social class, level of family acculturation, and, of course, personal preference.

Assimilation, Acculturation, and Cultural Pluralism

Often used interchangeably, the terms assimilation and acculturation are not synonymous. *Assimilation* is a process by which a new group (or individual) becomes part of the dominant culture, either through gradual disappearance of the differences which distinguish the two groups, or the cultural patterns of the new groups becoming part of the dominant culture. *Acculturation* is the first stage in this process in which characteristics of the dominant group are adopted by the new group (Gollnick & Chinn, 1994). In reality, many groups are not allowed to assimilate into the dominant culture and, therefore, maintain their own unique communities and cultural patterns. This is referred to as *cultural pluralism*. Cultural enclaves such as Chinatown, Little Italy, and East Los Angeles are examples of communities that have maintained their cultural identities.

Culture is Learned

We are born into a certain culture. Young children learn how to behave, what to value and believe, and about roles and relationships through observation, participation, and interaction with their families and communities. For example, at an early age, children learn what is expected of their gender role in their families and community. Some families give toy guns, cars, and balls to boys and give dolls and tea sets to girls.

Mainstream culture stress daily schedules when meals, naps, and toileting should occur at certain times of the day. In other cultures, children are fed when they are hungry, and fall asleep when they are tired, often sharing a bed with family members (Gonzalez-Mena, 1993).

In a preschool program, what we may regard as common expectations for children—acceptable play and social behaviors, appropriate communication styles, proper discipline procedures, and typical food and dress—may be unfamiliar to some children and their families.

Culture is Shared

We are part of an identifiable group because of shared values, beliefs, behaviors, preferences, and practices. Each dimension of culture—nationality, language, age, gender, family status, profession, geographic location, and socioeconomic status—influences each individual's cultural identity. For example, the shared values of upper- and middle-class people in southern California differ from their counterparts in Alaska. Each profession has its own culture. Service providers in early childhood education share a common belief in the importance and influence of early learning experiences in a child's development. Consider what you believe is important in a preschool program and how you can apply these values to your practices.

Culture is an Adaptation

Some cultural practices are adaptations to the requirements of the physical environment. Weather conditions
influence buildings, clothing styles, foods, and work
schedules. San Francisco has fewer homes with air con-
ditioners compared to homes in Los Angeles. Teachers
and preschoolers in Hawaii may go barefoot on the playground, but this is unacceptable in schools in New York
City. In countries with warm climates, stores and busi-
nesses may close for a few hours at midday during the
heat of the day. Further, an individual's cultural identity
may adapt because of changes in geographic location,
profession, educational level, and socioeconomic status.
Consider how your own values and beliefs regarding
child rearing and how children learn have been influenced by your role as an early childhood educator.

Culture is Dynamic

The artifacts of culture are subjected to change over
time. The clothing and hair styles of the 1960s are con-
siderably different from current styles. The music of
your parents' generation is different from yours, as are
the musical tastes of today's adolescents (Gollnick &
Chinn, 1994). Consider how your values, preferences,
and practices have changed over time and with experience. Also consider how the goals of early childhood
programs have changed from the optional, enrichment

goals of nursery schools in the 1950s, to the very essential day-care and educational goals of the 1990s.

Culture is Demonstrated in Values

Cultural values are those behaviors and ideas a particular group considers desirable and important. Some cultures place significant value on education; others emphasize friendship or family loyalty; and still others place great value on material possessions. At an early age, children observe and learn what is valued in their families and community, and they learn that if they possess what is valued in their culture, they will receive approval and prestige.

For some children, the values of their home culture may conflict with those of the cultural values of their preschool setting. For example, a family may encourage physical confrontation by boys when dealing with insults or hurt feelings. It is important to acknowledge these values in a nonjudgemental way while asserting that, in the preschool setting, aggressive behavior is forbidden. As a professional, consider how you might acknowledge the values of the home while maintaining the values of the setting in which you work where certain behaviors are unacceptable.

Another example is that of a preschooler whose family culture places great value in gold jewelry. Her new earrings are a great source of pride (Rothenberg, 1995), but you may be uncomfortable with her wearing expensive jewelry in the classroom. If you do not value jewelry, or if you disapprove of pierced ears on a child, your subtle or direct disapproval may confuse or hurt the child. Professionals should make an effort to view situations from the family's perspective in an effort to develop an understanding of their point of view. The challenge for today's early childhood educator is to balance the values of the home with the philosophy and practices of the preschool. Consider how you can learn about the values of families in your program and share information about your early childhood program with them.

Culture is Demonstrated in Nonverbal Communication

Each cultural group has its own means of communicating nonverbally such as with gestures and facial expressions. Some gestures in one culture can have different meanings in another (Axtell, 1991; Dresser, 1996). For example, in the United States, we interpret head nodding as a sign of agreement whereas among Asian, Native American, and Middle Eastern people, head nodding does not indicate understanding or agreement but rather that the listener *hears* the speaker (Lynch, 1998).

Gesturing to a child to come to you with your forefinger pointed upward is an obscene gesture among some Asian groups and our accepted hand signals for "OK" and "Good Job" offend some families from other countries. Physical contact is an area where there can be significant cultural differences. Some cultures practice physical contact whereas others do not. Children from Hispanic, French, and Italian backgrounds are said to be from "contact" cultures in which hugging, touching others, and being touched is typical behavior. In contrast, most Asians are not part of a contact culture, and hugging may be uncomfortable for a child from such a culture. However, acculturation has an influence. A fifth-generation, acculturated Asian American child may experience a good deal of physical affection and contact at home, and may welcome these signs of affection from others at preschool.

Misinterpretations of body language and gestures can lead to discomfort or conflicts among families, children, and teachers. As a professional in early childhood education, you should find out about children and families' typical nonverbal communication and help them understand those gestures used in your program.

Language is a Demonstration of Culture

Cultures differ in how information is conveyed. In "high context" cultures (Asian, African American, Arab, Hispanic, Native American), much of the information is conveyed through physical context, shared knowledge, and past experiences instead of by specific verbal messages. Communication is nonverbal and indirect. In "low context" cultures (North American, German, Scandinavian, Swiss), most of message are communicated verbally (Chen, Brekken, & Chan, 1997; Chen, Chan, & Brekken, 2000; Lynch, 1998).

Each culture has it own unique words and meanings. In some instances, there is no exact English equivalent and there are sounds in the English language not present in the child's home language. If the child has never heard particular sounds, imitating certain words can be a challenge. Even when English is spoken at home, the language may be used in many different ways, depending on the culture of the speaker, and the child may not be familiar with certain words or the ways in which they are used. For example, in preschool, children are expected to sing songs, play word games, answer questions about stories, and engage in problem-solving certain situations. At home, some children may be accustomed to a less play-oriented environment or a less-conversation interaction with adults.

Culture is Demonstrated in Many Other Ways

Our sense of time, causality, perceptions, and everyday habits are culturally determined. As you go through your daily routine, consider when, what, and how you eat; how, where, and when you bathe; and when, where, and how you sleep as all being influenced by your culture.

Challenges of a Diverse Society

The increasing diversity of the United States requires a pluralistic view that recognizes the mutual benefits and contributions of the multiple cultures of the country (Hanson, 1998). Many of us believe that the diversity of the United States enriches the social fabric of our communities. At the same time, cultural pluralism creates unique challenges that contribute to some of our current social problems. Some of us maintain or develop an ethnocentric point of view. *Ethnocentrism* is the inability of an individual to view another ethnic group as equal or valid members of society. Ethnocentrism may lead to biased attitudes and racist behaviors. We all view the world from our own cultural perspective. This is an automatic tendency. One significant challenge for educators in the twenty-first century is to learn about the cultures of others, and the range of behaviors and values that reflect these cultures. Perhaps the more difficult challenge, however, is to learn to understand our own culture; that is, why we do the things we do or think the way we think, and to understand where our biases lay.

Many of the social problems such as racism and social unrest that contributed to the Los Angeles riots in 1992 can be traced, in part, to cultural differences. For example, in the Korean cultural tradition, behaviors such as eye contact, smiling, and body contact may be considered disrespectful. The behaviors of Korean store owners may be interpreted as prejudiced and disrespectful by non-Korean customers as a Korean cashier may consider it polite to place money on the counter instead of into a customer's hand because body contact with strangers, especially members of the opposite sex, is not allowed. Also, and contrary to American cultural norms, smiling is considered thoughtless and shallow (Dresser, 1996), and direct eye contact may be considered rude and aggressive.

Living harmoniously in a culturally diverse society requires us to take the perspective of the other individual instead of looking at the world solely through our own cultural eyes. For example, try to take the point of view of the children in your class whose cultural backgrounds may differ from your own. For example, you notice that when you talk to two preschoolers in your class, they look down at the floor and not at you. Perhaps it is because these children are from traditional Mexican and Korean families and

have been taught to avoid eye contact as a sign of respect for those in authority. Eventually, as you establish a close relationship with them, explain to them, and to their families, in a gentle and respectful way, that in the United States, eye contact is a sign of interest and respect and lack of eye contact is considered disrespectful. Although it is important to respect diverse cultural values and practices, teachers should seek opportunities to share information with families and to prepare children for the expectations of the larger community.

Socioeconomic Disparity. Our society allows us to participate in a free enterprise system. Although we view this system as a strength, it often results in economic disparity. Some individuals have great wealth; many have moderate incomes and comfortably; others receive welfare; and some are homeless. These extremes intensified in the 1980s when the wealthy became wealthier and the poor became poorer. Poverty affects the lives of many children. Every month, more than 39 thousand children are born into poverty. More than 12 million of our children—one out of every five—are poor; and every night, 100 thousand children go to sleep homeless (Children's Defense Fund, 1991). Poverty alienates people from the rest of society and creates a culture of its own. The dominant middle class tends to have stereotypical attitudes about those living in poverty such as the belief that poor people are responsible for their economic situations because they have too many children, do not work, do not go to school, or take drugs. It is important that early childhood teachers resist such stereotypes.

Freedom of Religion. The growing number of immigrants arriving in the United States has contributed to the religious diversity of the nation. At the same time, religious beliefs influence the social and ethical agenda. Clashes between opposing groups on issues such as abortion and textbook censorship lead to spirited debates and even violence. Further, particular religious beliefs and practices may conflict significantly with current school policies. For example, primary age children who have been formally initiated into the Khalsa Sikh religious community must wear a knife, or *kirpan* (one of the five holy symbols), close to the body. In 1994, the U.S. Ninth Circuit Court of Appeals upheld the Sikh's right to practice their religious beliefs by wearing the *kirpan* at school, as long as the knife is blunted and sewn into its sheath for safety (Dresser, 1996). Consider what accommodations might be needed to serve children and families from different religious backgrounds in your preschool program.

❖ ELEMENTS OF CULTURE

The Macroculture

Although we live in a culturally diverse country, we share a common *macroculture*, the dominant or core culture of the United States. Our macro-American culture is characterized by the following values (Chan, 1998; Gollnick & Chinn, 1994; Zuniga, 1998):

- individualism and privacy
- equality
- industriousness
- ambition
- competitiveness
- self-reliance
- independence
- appreciation of the good life
- perception that humans are separate and superior in nature

The macroculture of the United States is described as an "individualistic culture" whereas other cultures are considered "collectivistic." Cultures with an individualistic orientation emphasize the potential, goals, achievements, and self-fulfillment of individuals. Collectivistic cultures view the needs of the group as having priority over those of the individual, and stress interdependence and cooperation for the collective good (Chan, 1998; Kohis, 1994; Zuniga, 1998).

Teachers of preschool children should consider how much the core values of our individualistic culture influence the preschool learning environment and expectations for children. How do these contrast with the collectivist values of other cultures? Review the following continuum of values, and identify your own beliefs, program expectations, and the values of families.

Values of Individualist Cultures	vs	Values of Collectivist Cultures
Mastery over nature		Harmony with nature
Personal control		Accepting fate
Doing		Being
Focused on future		Guided by past
Open to change		Respects tradition
Time dominates		Personal interaction dominates
Human equality		Hierarchy, rank, status
Youth oriented		Elders are influential
Self-help		Birthright inheritance
Independence, individualism		Interdependence, group welfare
Competition		Cooperation
Informality		Formality
Directness, openness, honesty		Indirectness, ritual, "saving face"
Low-context/high-verbal communication		High-context/low-verbal communication

Mainstream

In this text, the term *mainstream* refers to those individuals or groups who share values of the dominant culture. These are primarily members of the middle class who hold the values of the macroculture in the United States and are not limited to individuals from a single ethnic or racial group.

Microculture

Every society has subcultures or subcultural groups with unique cultural patterns which are not in common with the macroculture. The United States, with its pluralistic nature, has many microcultures. An individual's cultural identity is composed of traits and values transmitted by microcultures based on ethnicity, gender, social class, religion, age, primary language, geographic location (Gollnick & Chinn, 1994), and other dimensions including professional and marital status. Some of these cultural dimensions are primary characteristics with which we are born or which cannot be changed easily (age, race, gender, ethnicity, ability and disability, and sexual orientation); others are secondary dimensions we acquire throughout life (primary language, geographic location, religion, family status, education, work experience, profession, and income) (Loden & Rosener, 1991). Understanding that cultural identity is extremely complex helps us appreciate the diversity of our country and the families and children in our programs.

Children in your preschool program belong to many different microcultures. It is important to recognize that children may be different even when their backgrounds are similar. Although two children are Mexican Americans, middle class, and Roman Catholics, they may be different in the way they perceive things and in the ways they behave. If one child is a boy and the other a girl, the boy may be socialized differently from the girl. If both children are the same sex, they still can be different because one family may have traditional Mexican values whereas the other has become acculturated into the mainstream culture.

Race

Race categorizes people according to physical characteristics such as skin color, body size and shape, facial features, and hair texture. These characteristics result in four traditional labels: white or Caucasoid (Europeans); red (Native Americans); dark or Mongoloid/ Malayan (Asians and Pacific Islanders); and black or Negroid (Africans). Contemporary biologists and anthropologists reject race as a category because there is more genetic variation within racial groups than between them (Zuckerman, 1990). Moreover, individuals of a given race vary in their ethnic and cultural backgrounds. However, many biases exist toward certain physical features because of history, depictions in the popular media, and stereotypical assumptions.

Ethnicity

Ethnicity is a primary dimension of culture and describes a common origin such as history, heritage, language, religion, and other cultural features. French identifies a person's culture or country of origin as France. German identifies those who immigrated from Germany or whose parents or ancestors did. However, ethnicity is a complex and multidimensional construct that encompasses both race and culture of origin (Phinney, 1996).

Terms can be confusing since different ethnic groups may be combined as one, particularly for census purposes. There are five federal classifications based on race and ethnicity (U.S. Department of Education, Office for Civil Rights, 1987): American Indian or Alaskan Native; Asian or Pacific Islander; Hispanic (regardless of race); black (not of Hispanic origin); and white (not of Hispanic origin). However, Asians include many ethnic groups from at least 15 different countries of three geographic areas (Chan, 1998): China, Japan, and Korea in East Asia; Cambodia, Laos, Vietnam, Burma, Thailand, Malaysia, Singapore, Indonesia, and the Philippines in Southeast Asia; and India, Pakistan, and Sri Lanka in South Asia. Additionally, these countries represent different religious orientations with Confucianism, Taoism, and Buddhism the primary ones. Similarly, Hispanics represent 26 separate nationalities and a variety of racial groups (Bruder, Anderson, Schultz, & Caldera, 1991). Consider the ethnicity of a child raised in the United States by a family who immigrated to this country from Peru, and whose great grand parents in turn had immigrated to Peru from Japan. Ethnicity exists as a dimension by which we organize ourselves and categorize others. Consider how our terminology has changed depending on age, time, ethnicity, and geographic location: Oriental became Asian; colored became black, then African American. Although the term Hispanic is used federally, certain groups from Central and South America prefer to be called Latino, the common category name in California. It is common to hear the term Anglo used to refer to individuals of European heritage in Texas and California among a large percentage of the Latino population, but white is more common nationally. *If you must use an ethnic category in interactions with families in your preschool, it is important to inquire what each person from a particular ethnicity prefers to be called.*

Ethnicity affects perceptions, attitudes, and behaviors. For example, traditional Chinese, Korean, Japanese, and Vietnamese cultures are influenced by Confucian philosophy. Children from these families are taught to respect authority figures. Even if they do not like or value a particular authority figure such as an aunt, uncle, or teacher, their parents insist that deference be shown to these adults. Consequently, Asian children seem to demonstrate more compliant and respectful behavior than children from some other cultures toward their teachers. The learned behavior of deference to authority in traditional Asian families is maintained throughout adulthood. As a result, Asian parents may not openly disagree with school recommendations and decisions that conflict with the home culture. In contrast, an Anglo-American child raised with the values of our individualistic macroculture may challenge the teacher's authority when focusing on his or her individual needs and goals. It is important to gather information from families about their values and their priorities for their children's learning and development. In this way, preschool staff can discuss the philosophy, practices, and recommendations of the program within the context of their values.

Gender

Gender identification begins at birth and plays a critical role in shaping behavior. In the past, children's books published pictures of women doing housework and engaged in occupations such as nursing, teaching, librarians, and secretaries. On the other hand, doctors, lawyers, pilots, firemen, policemen, and athletes were portrayed by men. Consequently, we saw few men in traditional female occupations, or vice versa. Only recently have books and other forms of media made an effort to be nonsexist. As a professional working with young children, you should avoid sexist behavior and teaching materials in order to promote genuine gender equity. An early childhood environment should allow children to express their interests without fear of gender-oriented ridicule. Boys may choose to play with dolls and girls may choose to play basketball. Boys may talk about growing up to become nurses and girls may aspire to become firefighters. However, these options can pose serious dilemmas and conflicts between traditional families and preschool settings. How can you resolve these conflicts? Acknowledge when there are conflicts between the families' cultural values and the classroom philosophy. Listen to their perspectives on traditional roles and share your own regarding the importance of self-expression, play, and opportunity. As

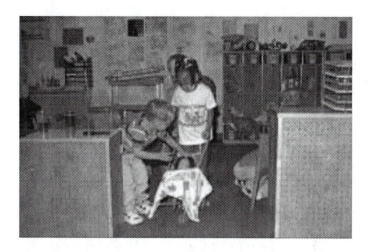

an early childhood educator, you should make every effort to build a relationship with the children's families through communication and a shared commitment to "doing what's best" for every child's development.

Socioeconomic Status

While differences exist across ethnic groups in North America, the greater differences in values, lifestyle, or behavior are found across social class categories. The everyday experiences of upper- and middle-class families such as reading books, playing on the computer, and participating in recreational outings are beyond the experience of families who live in poverty. These contrasting lifestyles of different social classes clearly influence the life experiences, socialization, perception, and behaviors of young children and their families. The home experiences of a child attending a Head Start program in an inner city area varies sharply from the home experiences of a child attending a private preschool program in a suburb. Their families' expectations of each preschool program vary as well. A teacher's expectation of what is part of preschoolers' home experiences should be based on the families' community. The preschool curriculum should be adapted to be meaningful and motivating for the children in the program. A story about a child learning to swim will only be understood if the child has seen a swimming pool and people swimming in it, if not in real life, then on television.

Further, teachers should identify community resources that families might use such as their local library, park, or recreation center. Although a family's socioeconomic status may influence its characteristics in certain predictable ways, teachers should be careful not to make stereotypical assumptions.

Religion

Although ethnicity, class, and gender are the three most frequently identified microcultural areas influencing a child's behavior and a family's expectations for that child, religion is a significant influence. Religion is considered very important to 58 percent of the population in the United States, and another 29 percent consider it fairly important. However, microcultural groups view the importance of religion differently. More females than males, more Southerners than Mid-Atlantic residents, more African Americans than whites, more people over 50 years old than those under 30 years of age, and more nonhigh-school graduates than college graduates view religion as very important in their lives (Bezilla, 1993). Religious practices influence child-rearing practices and other expectations families have for their children. As discussed previously, preschool staff should gather information about family values, priorities, and expectations for children in order to build a collaborative relationship with the family, and to provide a nurturing and meaningful program for the child.

Age

Age groups form microcultures. Consider the attitudes and perceptions of your parents about controversial issues such as interracial marriage, cohabitation of unmarried couples, and gay and lesbian lifestyles. How do their views compare to yours? How do your views compare to those of your grandparents? Preference for certain foods, clothing, hair styles, music, and other things are related as much to age group as to social class, gender, or ethnicity.

In addition to the influence of age on values, the variable of age is viewed differently by various cultures. These views influence expectations of, and behavior toward, children, adults, and the elderly and have important implications for early childhood service providers. For example, a preschooler may have few responsibilities in his or her family and, therefore, may be reluctant to help clean up at preschool. In another example, the eldest family member may be regarded as a key decision-maker, so it is important for grandparents to be included in parent conferences and other meetings. As an early childhood educator, you should become familiar with the particular age-related values of families that will influence your interactions with them and the preschoolers in your class. When you gather information about each family's composition, child rearing practices, and decision-making processes, you will gain insight into their age-related values.

Language

In 1994, approximately 2.6 million children in public school came from homes in which English was not the primary language, representing a 76 percent increase over the 1980s (Hornblower, 1995). One out of seven, or nearly 32 million people in the United States, use a language other than English at home (Haedden, 1995). Two out of three Head Start classrooms have children from at least two different first-language backgrounds and as many as 10 different home languages (Socio-Technical Research Applications, Inc., 1996). Today, it is estimated that there are 5.2 million preschoolers from homes that speak languages other than English (Kagan & Garcia, 1991).

In your preschool program, some children will have only limited English proficiency, others will have no English speaking skills, and others will speak English with nonstandard dialects such as Hawaiian pidgin, black English, or Jamaican patois. Language creates a common means of communication, security, and acceptance. Children who speak the same language or dialect may tend to interact mainly with each other. Imagine that you are four years old, in a strange or new situation, and surrounded by people you do not understand and who do not understand you. Imagine your relief, and reactions, if you hear another person speaking a language you can understand.

Although the issue of bilingual education remains a controversial and political one, preschool programs should identify strategies for establishing and maintaining communication with the child and family while working on the child's English skills. For example, through the use of bilingual staff, and by providing clear and comprehensible language input with visual supports. This will be discussed in detail in Chapter 5, Cultural Influences on Children's Communication Skills and Styles.

Geographic Region

There are significant cultural differences from one area of the country to another, and among rural, urban, and suburban settings. The values of a little boy growing up in southern California may be quite different from his peer living in Vermont. Similarly, the values of a four-year-old girl growing up in a Dallas suburb may vary from that of her counterpart raised in a rural community in Hunt county 55 miles away. Geographic location influences a family's values. Different geographical regions have different foods, customs, dialects, and environments. The combination of these factors make one region of the country vastly different from another and a family in your program who speaks English may face cultural adjustments if they have moved from another area of the country. Similarly, if you move to an unfamiliar community as a new professional, you may have to make cultural adjustments. Learning the culture of the community is an essential survival skill and enhances your ability to work effectively with young children and their families.

Disability

At least one child in ten has a special need that requires special education services. Given the movement toward inclusion of children with disabilities into programs for nondisabled children, it is likely you will have the opportunity to work with children with disabilities in your preschool class. These children benefit from being with nondisabled peers, and vice versa (Guralnick, 1990; Peck, Carlson, & Helmstetter, 1992). Families of children with disabilities sometimes form their own microculture because they share similar experiences, frustrations, and goals regarding services for their children. Parent and advocacy groups, mainly composed of members from the mainstream culture, often work for federal legislation and private funding to improve national and statewide services for children, young people, and adults with disabilities (Turnbull & Turnbull, 1997). As a preschool professional, you should gather information about the families' attitudes toward their children's disabilities. Some people who are deaf view their hearing loss as a cultural and linguistic difference instead of a disability. They prefer to be called "Deaf People" instead of "people who are deaf" because deafness is part of their identity and they communicate in American Sign Language. Some families may believe that children with disabilities are divine signs whereas others may experience deep feelings of loss or guilt. Each family's beliefs about the cause of their child's disability, their expectations for the child's development, and the child's participation in the community will influence their child-rearing practices (Deloache & Gottlieb, 2000; Groce & Zola, 1993; Lynch & Hanson, 1998) and their participation in your preschool program. For example, the mainstream value of working toward independent self-help skills for children who are disabled may conflict with a family's values of interdependence and family responsibility.

Stereotyping

Stereotypes are exaggerated generalities that often lead to dangerous oversimplifications. We all have them, and they influence how we interact with others. Preschool staff must examine the stereotypes they hold toward particular groups if they are to provide respectful and culturally responsive services to children and families from diverse backgrounds. These stereotypes can be challenged through personal interactions and by building relationships (Chen, Brekken, & Chan, 1997). It is a mistake to look at a Chinese American boy and make assumptions about his behavior and family values. If the child's mother is an ophthalmologist and the father a college professor, it is likely that the child will be more like the rest of his middle- and upper-class classmates, regardless of ethnicity, than the Southeast Asian child who has recently immigrated to this country with his family. You must take care to look at the whole child as a member of his or her family and community.

You may read vivid descriptions about the characteristics of families and children from various groups. Remember, the description is limited to the particular family situation. For example, a fourth-generation Portuguese American child whose great grandfather immigrated over forty years ago to fish in the waters off New England will be different from the child of a newly arrived Portuguese family. Moreover, the degree of a family's acculturation is "situational rather than absolute and can be modified to suit the needs of different kinds of cross-cultural encounters" (Green, 1982, p. 13). For example, a family from Mexico may choose to send their child to preschool to learn English, but speak Spanish and maintain traditional cultural practices at home.

Marisol and her Fajitas: A Story of Acculturation and Biculturalism

Marisol Baca is a preschooler who was born and raised in a traditional middle-class Mexican American family in a San Antonio, Texas, suburb. She attends a private preschool where the majority of students are white. There are three Asian Americans, a couple of other Hispanic children, and three African American students in the entire preschool. A

bright and observant four-year-old, Marisol has studied the children in her class carefully. She is aware that she is one of only two nonwhite children in her particular classroom. She knows what kinds of toys the other children like, what clothes they prefer, and what foods they eat. Whenever she has a choice, she selects the clothing, toys, and foods that the other children seem to value. Marisol is acculturating. She is taking on the trappings of the dominant group, and at the same time, allowing the cultural values of her home to become subordinate to those of her preschool class.

Marisol's favorite food are fajitas (marinated and broiled flank steak, sliced in strips). Knowing how much Marisol enjoys them, her mother packed some leftover fajitas for her lunch. When the other children, who were eating their sandwiches, noticed the fajitas, they asked Marisol what they were. Embarrassed because her lunch was so different from those of the other children, Marisol later asked her mother to fix her only sandwiches in the future. Confused, her mother responded, "But you love fajitas, Marisol." Marisol replied "No, I want sandwiches."

At the same time Marisol is acculturating, she is starting to reject some of the culture of her home. Children from diverse cultural backgrounds often see acculturation as a means to social acceptance. "If I am like the other children in the way I talk, eat, dress, think . . . if I listen to the same music and eat the same foods that they do, perhaps they will accept me even if I don't really look like them." Unfortunately, many of these children, without proper guidance, believe that as they acculturate, they must cast away the values and ways of their families as Marisol is trying to do. "I can't be both a real American and Mexican. I need to learn to speak English without an accent, so I won't speak Spanish anymore." Preschool teachers and other staff sometimes unwittingly encourage "Anglo conformity" which assumes the desirability of maintaining the mainstream cultural patterns and standards (Gordon, 1964).

Many children from diverse backgrounds can learn to be bicultural. They can become proficient in the mainstream culture, and, at the same time, maintain proficiency in the home culture. Later in life, these children, as bicultural or bilingual adults, will have social and professional advantages over those who can function in only one culture or language. Individuals who can function well in different cultural contexts usually have greater credibility in those cultures, greater acceptance, and increased job possibilities.

A competent early childhood educator should provide a learning environment that is nonthreatening to children from diverse backgrounds. In this way, children will learn to value the culture of their homes as well as that of the dominant culture.

In reality, had the children in the class been invited to taste Marisol's fajitas, many might have preferred their taste to that of their sandwiches. Marisol could have had her sandwiches and fajitas, too!

Understanding an individual's culture is often the key to understanding the individual. However, the key to being a successful early childhood professional in a diverse society lies not so much in learning about the characteristics of other cultures, but more in learning about your own culture and the ways in which it differs from that of the children and families whose lives you are trying to enhance.

As a professional working with young children, you will be part of one of the most exciting and challenging opportunities today. Classes and centers are no longer serving homogeneous groups of children. Like Jennifer Gregg, you will have children in your class whose beautiful and charming names will leave your tongue twisted as you first try to pronounce them correctly. Your life will be enriched as you discover cultures and values you did not realize existed. You might feel somewhat threatened at first, as nearly all of your colleagues have, as you face unfamiliar situations. However, you will have the exciting opportunity to learn and experience more than any early childhood professionals in any generation before. If you open your heart and mind, you will be exposed to the true riches of this important profession. As you learn about the children in your program and how to work effectively with them and their families, you will have the satisfaction of knowing that you indeed have made a great difference in their lives.

❖ REFERENCES

Axtell, R. E. (1991). Gestures: *The dos and taboos of body language around the world.* New York: John Wiley & Sons.
Bezilla, R. (Ed.). (1993). *Religion in America.* Princeton, NJ: Princeton Religion Research Center.

Bruder, M. B., Anderson, R., Schultz, G., & Caldera, M. (1991). Ninos especiales program: A culturally sensitive early intervention model. *Journal of Early Intervention, 15*(3), 268–277.

Chan, S. (1998). Families with Asian roots. In E. W. Lynch & M. J. Hanson (eds.), *Developing cross-cultural competence: A guide for working with young children and their families* (2nd ed.) (pp. 251–354). Baltimore: Paul H. Brookes Publishing.

Chen, D., Brekken, L., & Chan, S. (1997). *Project CRAFT: Culturally responsive and family focused training* [Video and booklet]. Baltimore: Paul H. Brookes Publishing.

Chen, D., Chan, S., & Brekken, L. (2000). *Conversations for three: Communicating through interpreters.* (Video and booklet). Baltimore: Paul H. Brookes Publishing.

Children's Defense Fund (1991). *The state of America's children.* Washington, DC: Author.

Deloache, J., & Gottlieb, A. (2000). *A world of babies. Imagined childcare guides for seven societies.* New York: Cambridge University Press.

Dresser, N. (1996). *Multicultural manners: New rules of etiquette for a changing society.* New York: John Wiley.

Gollnick, D. M., & Chinn, P. C. (1994). *Multicultural education in a pluralistic society* (4th ed.). Columbus, OH: Macmillan.

Gollnick, D. M., & Chinn, P. C. (1999). *Multicultural education in a pluralistic society* (5th ed). Columbus, OH: Merrill/Prentice Hall.

Gonzalez-Mena, J. (1993). *Multicultural issues in child care.* Mountain View, CA: Mayfield Publishing.

Goodenough, W. (1987). *Multicultural education in a pluralistic society* (4th ed.). Columbus, OH: Macmillan.

Gordon, M. M. (1964). *Assimilation in American life: The role of race, religion and national origins.* New York: Oxford University Press.

Green, J. W. (1982). *Cultural awareness in the human services.* Englewood Cliffs, NJ: Prentice Hall.

Groce, N. E., & Zola, I. K. (1993). Multiculturalism, chronic illness, and disability. *Pediatrics, 91,* 1048–1055.

Guralnick, M. J. (1990). Major accomplishments and future directions in early childhood mainstreaming. *Topics in Early Childhood Special education, 10*(2), 1–17.

Haedden, S. (1995, September 25). One nation, one language? *U.S. News & World Report, 119*(12), 38–42.

Hammer, T. J., & Turner, P. H. (1996). *Parenting in contemporary society.* Needham Heights, MA: Allyn & Bacon.

Hanson, M. J. (1998). Ethnic, cultural and language diversity in intervention settings. In E. W. Lynch & M. J. Hanson (eds.), *Developing cross-cultural competence: A guide for working with young children and their families* (2nd ed.) (pp. 3–22). Baltimore: Paul H. Brookes Publishing.

Hornblower, M. (1995, October 9). Putting tongues in check. *Time,* 40–50.

Kagan, S., & Garcia, E. (1991). Education of culturally and linguistically diverse preschoolers: Moving the agenda. *Early Childhood Research Quarterly, 6,* 427–443.

Knight, H. (1997, April 9). U.S. immigrant level at highest point since '30s. *Los Angeles Times*, pp. A1, A14.

Kohis, L. R. (1994). *The values Americans live by.* Washington, DC: Merifian House International.

Loden, M., & Rosener, J. (1991). *Workforce America!* Burr Ridge, IL: Business One Irwin.

Lynch, E. W. (1998). Developing cross-cultural competence. In E. W. Lynch and M. J. Hanson (eds.), *Developing cross-cultural competence. A guide for working with young children and their families* (2nd ed.) (pp.47–90). Baltimore: Paul H. Brookes Publishing.

Lynch, E. W., & Hanson, M. J. (1998). *Developing crosscultural competence: A guide for working with young children and their families* (2nd ed). Baltimore: Paul H. Brookes Publishing.

Peck, C. A., Carlson, P., & Helmstetter, E. (1992). Parent and teacher perceptions of outcomes for typically developing children in integrated early childhood programs: A statewide survey. *Journal of Early Intervention, 16*(1), 53–63.

Phinney, J. S. (1996). When we talk about American ethnic groups, what do we mean? *American Psychologist, 15*(9), 918–927.

Roof, W. C. (1990). Return of the baby boomers to organized religion. In C. H. Jaquet, Jr. (ed.), *1990 yearbook of American and Canadian churches.* Nashville, TN: Abingdon Press.

Rothenberg, B. A. (1995). *Understanding and working with parents and children from rural Mexico.* Menlo Park, CA: The CHC Center for Child and Family Development Press.

SocioTechnical Research Applications, Inc. (1996). *Report on the ACYF bilingual/multicultural survey.* Washington, DC: The Head Start Bureau.

Turnbull, A. P., & Turnbull, H. R. (1997). *Families, professionals and exceptionality* (3rd.ed). Upper Saddle River, NJ: Prentice Hall.

U.S. Department of Education, Office for Civil Rights (1987). *1986 elementary and secondary school civil rights survey: National summaries.* Washington, DC: DBS.

Zuckerman, M. (1990). Some dubious premises in research and theory on racial differences. *American Psychologist, 45,* 1297–1303.

Zuniga, M. E. (1998). Families with Latino roots. In E. W. Lynch and M. J. Hanson (eds.), *Developing cross-cultural competence. A guide for working with young children and their families* (2nd ed.) (pp. 209–250). Baltimore: Paul H. Brookes Publishing.

CHAPTER 2

Creating Culturally Responsive Early Childhood Environments

An early childhood setting is often the first formal learning environment young children experience that is different from being at home or with relatives and with family friends. All children have certain beliefs and behaviors taught in the home or family culture that may vary from those expected in the preschool environment. For example, four- year-old Mei-Mei Kwan has learned at home to be respectful to adults, to use their surnames and address them as Miss, Mr., or Mrs.; to speak only when spoken to, and to not question adults. She is confused by her teacher's behaviors at preschool. Her teacher wants the children to call her "Jennie" instead of Miss Gregg, and tries to engage Mei Mei in conversation. Mei-Mei finds this experience unusual and uncomfortable.

As an early childhood educator, you will have children from diverse backgrounds in your program and each child's comfort level will depend partly on the "fit" between the home and program culture. In the transactional model of development (Sameroff & Chandler, 1975), a child's developmental outcome is a consequence of the dynamic interplay between the social and physical environment and the child's abilities, temperament, and other attributes. A child's optimal development is supported when there is a good fit between the child's needs and abilities and what the environment expects and provides.

The art of providing a culturally-responsive preschool environment is a reciprocal and systematic process involving children, families, staff, and the cultures of the homes, program, and larger community. The goal of this chapter is to provide you with a framework within which you, as an early childhood professional, can examine your own personal beliefs and professional strengths and needs, evaluate program practices, and identify strategies for professional and program development related to providing culturally responsive early childhood education services.

❖ THE ROLE OF EARLY CHILDHOOD EDUCATION

Our contemporary lifestyles and values resulted in an increase in the number of young children in child care settings and early education programs. Some children have single working parents, whereas others have families in which both parents work outside the home. Many parents, even those who work in the home, now believe their young children benefit from group care or preschool experiences. Recent research supports the beneficial effects of high-quality day care for young children (Lacayo, 1997). In the United States, early childhood education occurs in a variety of settings for young children between birth and eight years of age. The National Association for the Education of Young Children (NAEYC) (1994) definition of early childhood settings includes Head Start programs, family day care, both private and public child care centers, nursery schools, prekindergarten programs, kindergarten programs, primary grades, and before- and after-school child care programs in elementary schools.

Early childhood programs for preschool age children in the United States have a variety of goals. Head Start was established in 1965 as the first preschool enrichment program to promote the development of three- and four-year-olds living in poverty in the United States (Day, 1983). State licensed day-care centers provide child care for working parents. There is sometimes a great variation in the quality of early childhood educational experiences in these centers. Private preschools, on the other hand, have a particular curriculum as their focus. For example, Montessori programs for three- to seven-year-olds provide specifically designed materials to promote self-help skills, language development, problem-solving, and concept development.

You may have children in your early childhood program whose families are relatively new to the United States, some of whom are familiar only with preschool programs in their countries of origin. Although public preschool education is valued, it probably was not an option for some families, or was not necessary because the mother did not work out of the home or because children were cared for by extended family members. However, in the United States, these families now must enroll their children in early childhood programs because of job requirements and the lack of extended family support. In addition, some families send their children to preschool to learn English and the customs of their new country.

Based on their cultural backgrounds and previous experiences, families have certain assumptions about an early childhood program. These expectations may or may not fit the program you provide. It is, therefore, important to discuss the philosophy and purpose of your particular program with the families and to elicit their questions about the program. In this way, families can develop a true understanding of what the program has to offer, make decisions about their children's learning experiences, and become involved in their children's early education.

Ask yourself . . .
- *In what type of early childhood setting are you working? For example, is it a day-care setting, nursery school, private or public preschool, Head Start, or other program?*
- *What is the primary goal or purpose of your early childhood program? For example, does it to provide day care for working families, provide children with early learning experiences to promote later success in school, develop children's early socialization, play, and language skills, or promote the children's overall development?*
- *What are the cultural, ethnic, and linguistic backgrounds of the program staff and the children and families served in the program? For example, are there bilingual/ bicultural staff to serve Latino, Vietnamese, and Russian families who do not speak English or to assist other program staff working with these children and families?*
- *How do you inform families about the philosophy, goals, and activities of your program and how do you get them involved? For example, do you provide written information in easy-to-read formats or hold family orientation meetings to introduce new families to your program?*

❖ **DEVELOPMENTALLY APPROPRIATE PRACTICE**

As a new professional in early childhood education, you are involved with your professional organization, the NAEYC. This professional organization identifies state-of-the-art and recommended practices in early childhood education including the concept of Developmentally Appropriate Practice (DAP). The standard of developmentally appropriate practice is the hallmark of early childhood education and is used for the accreditation process of early childhood programs through NAEYC (NAEYC 1984, 1991; Bredekamp & Copple, 1997).

DAP is extremely complicated and influenced not only by the culture of the program and community but also by the backgrounds, abilities, and interests of the children. It encompasses three aspects: age appropriateness, individual appropriateness, and cultural appropriateness (Ludlow & Berkeley, 1994; Phillips, 1994). There is no *one* right way to implement a developmentally appropriate program (see Mallory & New, 1994 for a discussion of the issues.) A true DAP early childhood setting provides a variety of experiences each child needs at a particular time (Kostelnik, 1992; NAEYC, 1996). The 1997 NAEYC statement of developmentally appropriate practices lists 12 principles. The sixth principle states the following: "Development and learning occur in and are influenced by multiple social and cultural contexts."

DAP settings are organized physical and social environments that support the learning needs of the children. Instruction occurs through planned activities to support children's learning in meeting specific educational goals. Every detail such as the physical setting, placement of furniture, type of materials, grouping of children, amount of time, role of the teacher, and expectations of the children should be orchestrated carefully. However, the teacher allows the children's curiosity, interests, and participation in planned activities to lead instruction in different directions to take advantage of "teachable moments" and incidental learning opportunities.

The principles of DAP involve identifying children's interests, providing motivating activities, and arranging the environment to encourage exploration. However, these practices may conflict with certain cultural values. For example, some families from traditional Asian backgrounds may have academic expectations for their preschoolers and not see the value of play and catering to the child's interests. It is important to explain the purpose of program activities to families and how these skills relate to later success in school.

As you read in Chapter 1, Jennifer Gregg has a diverse classroom of four-year-olds. Some of the children began the program as three-year-olds; others were new to the preschool. Several of the children came from cultural backgrounds different from Jennifer's as well as from each other, and some children spoke English, Spanish, or Vietnamese as their primary language. There was also a child in the class with Down syndrome. The children also represent a wide range of socioeconomic backgrounds.

Jennifer wants to create a developmentally appropriate program that meets the learning needs of each child. Clearly, the program must be flexible and still implement the guiding principles of DAP. Jennifer identifies each child's interests, provides motivating activities to build on these strengths, and structures the environment accordingly. However, some children are not comfortable with a "child centered" environment in which they are expected to initiate, explore and follow their own interests. They may need more adult direction, particularly at certain times. Also, despite the DAP emphasis on "process" rather than "products", some families are more interested in the products of their child's preschool experience than in the process of learning activities. These differences in the behaviors of the children and in the expectations of their families are related to their culture and values.

Ask yourself . . .
- *How do you define developmentally appropriate practice?*
- *Have you implemented developmentally appropriate practices in your program? How?*
- *What questions or concerns do you have about the implementation of developmentally appropriate practice with children from diverse cultural backgrounds in your program?*

❖ DEVELOPING A PROGRAM PHILOSOPHY

A cohesive early childhood program has a clearly defined philosophy concerning its purpose and role in the early development and learning of young children. A program philosophy comprises statements about the values and beliefs of early childhood education and significant characteristics about the teaching and learning processes. As an early childhood professional, you should be familiar with the program philosophy and participate in its original development and planned reviews. A program philosophy should be reviewed every few years to determine whether the statements are still valid and helpful, or if the philosophy needs to be revised to meet current values and practices. For example, does the program philosophy address the learning needs of *all* children in the program, including those from culturally and linguistically diverse backgrounds?

In addition, you should be able to articulate your teaching philosophy that reflects the values of the overall program and guides interactions with individual children and families. Then general program goals and specific instructional practices are developed, based on the program philosophy.

Ask yourself . . .

- *What are the stated philosophy, purpose, and goals of your program? Do they address the diverse needs of families and children?*
- *What is your teaching philosophy? Does it address different family priorities?*
- *What instructional practices and activities reflect the program philosophy and demonstrate commitment to*

program goals? Do they address diverse learning styles
and needs?
- What do you want children to learn? Do you have specific
  goals for young children from culturally and linguistically
  diverse backgrounds?
- How do you know what a family wants their child to
  learn? Do you have specific strategies for working with
  interpreters, for example?
- How do you resolve differences in your goals and expectations for children with those of their families? For example,
  what would you do if one family wanted their preschooler
  to work on academic skills in your play-based preschool
  program or if another felt strongly their male child should
  not play with dolls?

❖ MULTICULTURAL EDUCATION GOALS FOR EARLY CHILDHOOD PROGRAMS

Early childhood programs should be safe and nurturing learning environments that provide developmentally appropriate curriculum to promote all areas of
children's learning and development. At the same
time, the demographics of our society require the following goals of multicultural education (Kendell, 1983,
p. 3):

- to teach children to respect others' cultures and
  values as well as their own;
- to help all children function successfully in a
  multicultural, multiracial society;
- to develop a positive self-concept in those children most affected by racism, such as children of
  color;
- to help all children experience their differences as
  culturally diverse people and their similarities as
  human beings in positive ways; and
- to encourage children to experience people of diverse cultures working together as unique parts of
  a whole community.

These goals require early childhood programs that
not only support each child's self-esteem about his or
her own cultural and ethnic background but also provide accurate, practical, and respectful information
about diverse cultures of the local community.

Moreover, early childhood programs should provide a foundation for the skills that young children will need to succeed in later school and life experiences. Children should learn standard English and conventional manners to succeed in the mainstream culture. For example, although there is disagreement on the best strategy to help preschoolers develop bilingual skills (Chang, Muckelroy, & Pulido-Tobiassen, 1996), early childhood programs can support the continued development of young children's home languages while helping them acquire English (Wong Fillmore, 1991).

How and when to teach young children skills required in our mainstream culture is a dilemma for all early childhood teachers in the face of popular media, established attitudes, and prevalent practices. In the current era of "political correctness," you, as an early childhood professional, should consider carefully the dual goals of honoring each child's native culture and, at the same time, provide the foundation for success within the mainstream culture. You should discuss these issues with administrators, staff, and families to implement an effective program for meeting the learning needs of these children.

The natural curiosity of young children triggers questions about differences they see among peers such as language use, behavior, skin color, hair texture, and body size or weight. Some children make comments about what is "good" or "bad", "pretty" or "ugly." How do you respond to a child who makes a derogatory remark about another child's physical features, language, behavior, or abilities? Would you do some things differently next time? Do not ignore these questions or comments, or discourage a child from making such comments. Negative or punishing responses teach the child that topics related to language differences, skin color, or other physical characteristics are shameful or inappropriate and should not be discussed. As their teacher, you need to use these questions and comments as learning opportunities to build an appreciation of similarities, differences, and humanness (Chang, Muckelroy, & Pulido-Tobiassen, 1996; Derman-Sparks & the A.B.C. Task Force, 1989) . These situations challenge you to *go beyond* simply pointing out the effects of hurtful comments such as "You've hurt her feelings by calling her ugly", disciplining the child by saying,"Sit in that chair until you can think of something nice to say; you may not make fun of the way Carlos speaks", or by using platitudes such as "We are all beautiful." These responses may not help develop children's values and tolerance of differences.

Ask yourself . . .

* *How should you discuss similarities and differences in physical characteristics, language, abilities, and behaviors with the children?*

  —Celebrate the concept of "difference". Instead of looking for similarities or identifying the object that "doesn't fit", include activities where children notice all the wonderful differences in leaf patterns and colors, shapes of rocks, people's hair color, species of birds, and so-on.

  —Read stories that feature children with a wide range of abilities and disabilities and who come from diverse backgrounds, family compositions, social class, and communities.

  —Ask questions that encourage children to identify differences from their own situations and similarities with other children and families.

  —If your classroom staff is not bilingual/bicultural, identify other adults (from families or community resources) who can serve as role models, read stories, and develop other language learning and cultural activities.

* *How do you provide information about, and build pride in, the different cultures, ethnicities, languages, and lifestyles represented in your program?*

  —Investigate curricular resources such as the Anti-bias Curriculum (Derman-Sparks & A.B.C. Task Force, 1989), Roots & wings: Affirming culture in early childhood programs (York, 1991), the following chapters in this book, and other related literature (Gonzalez-Mena, 1993; Chang, Muckelroy, & Pulido-Tobiassen, 1996) as starting points to develop your culturally responsive program.

  —Include music, songs, dances, instruments, games, and chants from various cultures as regular components of your program activities. Discuss them with the children and have fun.

  —Invite families to contribute to the activities around different cultures and draw on the resources of the community.

- *How do you teach children about the conventional behavior of the mainstream culture?*
  —Discuss your questions, concerns, and goals for creating a culturally responsive program that teaches children the skills they need for later school success with your colleagues and program administrator.
  —Identify the skills children need to succeed in kindergarten or their next learning environment. Develop a plan for the program as a whole, share it with families, and involve them in the process of developing relevant activities and identifying appropriate materials and other resources.
- *How do you counter the stereotypes perpetuated by the popular media and established practices?*
  —Monitor common songs, games, and chants that perpetuate inconsiderate and hurtful attitudes ("Ten Little Indians;""Eenie, meenie, mynie, mo;" "Ching Chong Chinaman").
  —Provide photographs, magazines, books, and other visual materials that are authentic representations of the diversity of cultures in your program.
  —Provide play materials such as dress-up clothing, dolls, miniatures, puzzles, and arts and crafts materials that reflect and encourage a celebration of cultural diversity. Shy away from stereotypical materials such as feathered headbands and toy tomahawks that represent Native Americans.
  —Develop a relationship with community organizations that represent the variety of cultures of the children in

your program. Use these organizations as resources to obtain information about stories, songs, music, games, celebrations, and other customs.

❖ DEVELOPING CROSS-CULTURAL COMPETENCE

Cross-cultural competence refers to "ways of thinking and behaving that enable members of one cultural, ethnic, or linguistic group to work effectively with members of another" (Lynch & Hanson, 1992, p. 356). Cultural sensitivity, cultural responsiveness, ethnic competence, intercultural competence, and intercultural effectiveness are related terms that convey a similar meaning. Today, developing cross-cultural competence is a professional standard and is related to NAEYC- identified critical professional competencies in early education: (a) providing learning opportunities that promotes each child's development; (b) recognizing and understanding the child as part of a family, culture, and society; and (c) developing and maintaining collaborative relationships with families(1994).

To develop cross-cultural competence, you must start a process of self-reflection, gather information about your own culture and that of others, appreciate cultural similarities and differences, use cultural re-

sources, and acknowledge the value of all cultures (Green, 1982; Lynch & Hanson, 1998; Turnbull & Turnbull, 1996). To begin this lifelong process, you should have a sense of self, a degree of maturity, and a commitment to providing culturally responsive programs.

Ask yourself . . .

- *How do you find out about the family, community, and other aspects of the environment that contribute to a specific child's development? For example, does your program have a family interview process?*
- *How do you provide essential learning opportunities for children within the context of their families and cultures? Do you adapt activities to include objects or materials that are familiar to children from diverse cultural backgrounds, for example, in cooking activities?*
- *How do you build collaborative relationships with families, especially those from diverse backgrounds? For example, do you communicate with the primary decision-maker in the family? Have you learned some key phrases in the family's preferred language?*

❖ DEVELOPING AN AWARENESS OF YOUR OWN CULTURE

Take a moment and look over the following 18 points. Simply read each statement and answer whether you would tend more to agree or to disagree with each one.

1. Infants should sleep in their own bed.
2. Infants should be placed on the floor to encourage motor milestones such as rolling over and crawling.
3. Infants should be allowed to explore and have the opportunity to engage in trial and error.
4. Infants should be weaned from the bottle by age two or earlier.
5. Infants should be encouraged to finger feed, even if it messy.
6. Speaking to young children supports the development of language and cognitive skills.
7. Encouraging young children to describe things and tell stories is important.

8. A preschool age child should be able to carry on a conversation with an adult.
9. Adults should respond to children's questions.
10. Physical punishment is never appropriate for young children.
11. Children should be given explanations for rules and consequences of negative behavior.
12. Gender stereotypes should be avoided in children's toys, and storybooks; adult expectations of behaviors of boys and girls should be the same.
13. A child who avoids eye contact and interaction with adults may have an emotional problem.
14. A preschool child who rarely pretends or plays with toys, and prefers teasing and roughhousing, should be referred for an evaluation.
15. A preschool child who prefers to play alone has difficulty with development of social skills.
16. Discipline should always be fair; all children in a class or family should be treated equally.
17. A child should be allowed to explain why he or she did something wrong.
18. A preschool child is much too young to handle the responsibility of caring for an infant or toddler.

Most likely, you tended to agree with all the statements listed. However, as will be discussed in greater detail in Chapter 3, caregivers in other cultures may strongly *disagree* with many of these statements.

We cannot become culturally competent service providers without first understanding our own culture, especially the values and biases we bring to our work. Developing an awareness of our own culture is the first step toward providing a culturally responsive learning environment for young children from diverse backgrounds. Each of us has values, beliefs, and assumptions that reflect our life experiences. As discussed in Chapter 1, our cultural identities are composed of beliefs transmitted by belonging to various microcultures (Gollnick & Chinn, 1994; Loden & Rosener, 1991).

It is important to recognize that your professional knowledge and skills, as well as your personal life experiences, influence your beliefs about early education and your interactions with the children and families in your program. Begin your development of cross-cultural competence by identifying your membership in the various microcultural groups and that most influence your perspective on early childhood education. Examine your own culture and experience with regard to each of the following factors:

Age
Gender
Ethnicity
Nationality
Language(s)
Religion
Geographic Location
Educational Level
Marital Status
Parental Status
Ability/Disability
Socioeconomic Status

Think about Jennifer Gregg, the new preschool teacher you met in Chapter 1. She is a 21-year-old single woman born and raised in a middle-class Anglo-European family in a rural community of central California. She just moved to the Los Angeles area and began her first job in a preschool program at a state university.

Irene Gavin is also a new teacher at the same university preschool. She has relocated to the Los Angeles area after living most of her life in Louisiana because of her husband's job as an attorney with the Federal Trade Commission. Irene is a 40-year-old African American woman who has four children and a master's degree in early education. Although Irene and Jennifer are team teaching in the same classroom, they had very different life experiences that influence their beliefs about and expectations of the children in their program. For example, Jennifer Gregg is concerned that two African American boys seem aggressive and hyperactive. She wonders if they should be evaluated. Irene Gavin does not consider the boys' behavior to be problematic and enjoys their exuberance.

Role of the Family

In our mainstream culture, we expect families to become involved with their children's early childhood programs. Collaboration and partnership with families

are quality indicators of early childhood programs. However, these concepts are foreign to many families who consider program staff the experts; they are not used to being involved in their children's education and they may question the teacher's competency if you seem to rely on their opinions rather than on your own professional judgement.

It is essential to explain the program's philosophy of parent participation and family involvement, and that these are valued practices in the United States. Some families are comfortable expressing disagreement with program practices, make direct requests, and are very clear about their expectations. For example, in a preschool program that has a daily painting activity, Mrs. Hunter asked the preschool staff to make sure her daughter, Laura, did not get any paint on her clothing. Mr. and Mrs. Kwan also are concerned that their daughter, Mei-Mei, came home with paint on her clothing. They do not understand why the school allows the children to spend so much time painting when they need to learn how to read and write.

However, the Kwans did not express their concerns to the staff because in their culture; this would be disrespectful. It requires a great deal of time, effort, trust, and communication to build a collaborative relationship with any family. When the family has a cultural background or language different from your own, establishing this relationship takes even more care and effort.

Ask yourself . . .
- *How can you let families know what you expect of their children in your program? For example, do you hold a family orientation meeting during which you explain the program and show sample activities on a video?*
- *How can you let families know about the importance of their participation and involvement in your program?*
- *How can you tailor your expectations and requirements for family involvement to meet the concerns, priorities, and resources of individual families? For example, are there a variety of options for family participation, and is every type of contact valued and respected?*

Differences in Child-Rearing Practices

Everyone has an opinion about the best way to care for infants and young children, and provide for their early learning experiences. Beliefs about child rearing practices are influenced by many of the dimensions discussed in the previous section including age, ethnicity, religion, occupation, geographic location, religion, and socioeconomic status. As an early childhood professional, you should recognize how your own upbringing and personal experiences influence your child-rearing values and practices. Take this opportunity to gather information about your heritage and appreciate your family's cultural journey (Lynch & Hanson, 1998). Talk to older family members to find out what they know about your family history. Think about the stories you heard growing up in your family, particularly regarding your experiences as a young child.

Ask yourself . . .
- *How did your family expect you to behave at the dinner table, in the grocery store, and in other situations at home and in the community?*

- *As a young child, what were your responsibilities in your family? Did they expect you to take care of younger siblings, feed pets, put your toys away after play, or help with household tasks?*
- *As a child, how did you interact with adults? For example, did you address nonfamily members by their first names or as Mr., Mrs., and Miss? Did they expect you "to be seen and not heard" and did you engage in informal conversation with adults?*
- *What were your parents' methods of discipline?*
- *What types of games and activities did you play with other children?*
- *What types of toys did you have?*

Now that you have a clear recollection of your life as a young child, think about the young children you know today; they may be your own or those of friends or relatives.

Ask yourself . . .
- *How do you expect these children to behave at the dinner table, in the grocery store, and in other situations at home and in the community?*
- *What responsibilities do these children have in their family? Do their families expect them to take care of younger siblings, feed pets, put their toys away after play, or help with household tasks?*
- *How do they interact with adults? Do they address nonfamily members by their first names or as Mr., Mrs., and Miss? Does the family expect them "to be seen and not heard" and do they engage in informal conversation with adults?*
- *How are these children disciplined?*
- *What types of games and activities do they play with other children?*
- *What types of toys do they have?*

When you have a clear idea about your own culture, beliefs, and values, you can appreciate the cultural perspectives of the children and families in your program. Identify the various ways you can get to know each family better. Consider the similarities and differences between the way a particular family views the world and your own worldview.

Families have different perspectives on family responsibilities, on child-rearing practices, expectations for their children, and for the early childhood program. These perspectives will influence your relationship with the children and their families.

Think about the children in your program.

Ask yourself . . .
- *How do the parents expect their children to behave at the dinner table, in the grocery store, and in other situations at home and in the community?*
- *What responsibilities do these children have in their family? Do their families expect them to take care of younger siblings, feed pets, put their toys away after play, or help with household tasks?*
- *How do they interact with adults? Do they address non-family members by their first names or as Mr., Mrs., and Miss? Does the family expect them "to be seen and not heard" and do they engage in informal conversation with adults?*
- *How are these children disciplined?*
- *What types of games and activities do they play with other children?*
- *What types of toys do they have?*

Child-rearing practices in our mainstream culture are related to the individualistic orientation of the United States which stresses independence (Lynch & Hanson, 1992). Newborns are expected to sleep alone, toddlers are expected to feed themselves, and preschoolers are encouraged to be competitive and to do the best they can. As mentioned in Chapter 1, families from a traditional collectivist culture emphasize interdependence and the cooperation of the group as a whole. The family sleeps together, self-feeding occurs at a later age than in individualistic cultures, and being competitive—to stand apart from the group—is considered inappropriate and shameful behavior.

Chapter 3, "Understanding Cultural Differences in Family Child-Rearing Practices," provides information on culture-specific influences on child-rearing. Remember, what you read and hear about specific cultural groups are general trends and do not apply to every family from that culture. You should find out, by asking the family, whether what you learned about a particular culture relates to them or is helpful information for understanding their child.

Developmental Expectations

What young children learn in an early childhood settings is influenced by the expectations of their teachers. It is important that you are aware of unconscious preconceptions and negative stereotypes that may influence your expectation of a child and your interpretation of his or her behavior. For example, Mei-Mei Kwan is a small Chinese-American girl who wears glasses. Jennifer Gregg expected her to be a quiet child who follows all the rules. Jennifer is surprised that Mei-Mei is a very active, talkative, and social preschooler who constantly needs reminding of the classroom rules.

Developmental expectations are influenced not only by your culture and the community but also by your own training and contact with young children. You acquired knowledge related to what is expected of children at certain ages. However, developmental milestones become meaningful only in the context of the values and expectations of the family and community in which *the child* is raised (Bowman & Stott, 1994; Carlson & Harwood, 2000). For example, a study by Schulze, Harwood, Goebel, & Schubert (1999) compared the developmental expectations of specific milestones for three groups of mothers (Anglo, Puerto Rican, and Filipino). They found that the age at which infants were expected to sleep through the night ranged from 11 months (Anglo mothers) to 32 months (Filipino mothers).

We must be aware of cultural influences on what we consider developmentally appropriate so that our expectations are reexamined within the context of the child's background. Chapter 4, "Cultural Influences on Young Children's Social Skills and Behaviors," is one resource. As discussed previously, our mainstream cultural emphasis on autonomy and independence is not a universal value. In addition, the child's familiarity with early childhood materials and the environment also should be considered. A child's lack of experience with certain situations results in him or her not knowing what to do. If a child has not played on outdoor equipment, he or she may appear timid or clumsy when climbing up on the slide or getting on the swings. Similarly, if a child is unfamiliar with many of

the toys and materials in the room, he or she may
seem unruly or hyperactive when exploring and manipulating the materials. As a result of cultural differences and misinterpretations, an early childhood
professional may misunderstand a child's behavior, un-
derestimate a child's ability, and provide inappropriate
learning experiences (Bowman & Stott, 1994). In order
to provide new and meaningful learning experiences,
you should seek to understand what children experience at home and in their communities, and how
those experiences are organized.

Ask yourself . . .
- *How do you obtain information about the children's activ-*
  ities at home, and their previous and current experiences
  in other environments? For example, does your program
  include opportunities for home visits and for interviews
  with families?
- *How do you support a child who is totally unfamiliar with*
  the activities, materials, and equipment of your program?
  For example, do you have a systematic and individualized
  approach for orienting a new child to your program such
  as assigning the child a "buddy" (a paraprofessional or
  older student) who is from the same cultural/linguistic
  background as the child.
- *How do you introduce new materials and activities to the*
  children? For example, do you demonstrate expected
  behaviors and new activities?

Conflicts Between Home and Program

Differences in practices and expectations between the
home and early childhood settings may result in conflicts between families and programs, with the children
caught in the middle. Your early childhood program is
likely to have mainstream expectations regarding the development of independence and autonomy in feeding,
toilet training, and sleeping (Gonzalez-Mena, 1993). You
encourage your toddlers to begin to feed themselves,
drink from a cup, become toilet trained, and sleep alone.
Certainly, you expect that these skills are accomplished.
However, independence in these skills may not be the
expectations for children in the home setting. Similarly,
a program's focus on "hands-on" and active play may

conflict with a family's expectation of learning academic skills at preschool. Conflicts between homes and programs should be viewed as professional development opportunities to refine reflection, communication, problem-solving, and negotiation skills.

You can help children (and parents) learn that certain behaviors are appropriate for specific contexts, and learn the behavior and skills expected by the dominant culture. For example, children should be quiet in the grocery store but not on the playground; or they must walk inside the school building but can run outside on the playground. If children understand that certain behaviors are appropriate at home and others are appropriate at school, they are more likely to reconcile the differences between their experiences at home and at school (Phillips, 1994).

Remember that caregiving and other practices related to young children are determined by cultural values which may change over time. For example, breastfeeding very young children and families sharing a common bed are customary in many cultures whereas they are historically controversial in our society. Currently, in the 1990s, breastfeeding is widely accepted as beneficial to the infant and mother in our mainstream culture, and the notion of a family bed viewed less negatively (Wright, 1997). It is important to realize that there are many equally valid ways to accomplish the task of healthy child rearing.

Gonzales-Mena (1992, 1993) has identified four possible ways of resolving conflicts in child-rearing practices between home and center:

1. The issue is *not* resolved because neither program nor family will change their positions. If neither the family nor the program understand the others' point of view, conflicts may not be resolved.
2. The issue is resolved by the program changing to accommodate the family's perspective.
3. The issue is resolved by the family changing to accommodate the program's perspective.
4. The issue is resolved through compromise by each side viewing the other's perspective.

Consider the possible outcomes for the situation below:

Lisa

Lisa is four years old and has been in your preschool for the past three weeks. She wears beautiful hand-made dresses to the center and observes other children instead of participating in play activities. Her parents do not want her to get dirty and ruin her clothes. Your program encourages active play outdoors, water play, and art activities. You believe that Lisa needs to develop age-appropriate play and social skills, and the program activities are developmentally appropriate and intended for these goals.

Ask yourself . . .

- *How would you share this situation with a mentor or colleague for assistance in your process of reflection and problem-solving ?*
- *As Lisa's teacher, what strategies would you use to understand the family's perspective and their goals for, and concerns about, Lisa?*
- *How would you talk to the family about your teaching philosophy, program goals, and your beliefs about Lisa's learning needs?*

Possible Outcomes

Suppose that in the family's religion, community, and culture, girls are expected to wear dresses and to be clean and well-behaved in public. Clearly, these cultural values and expectations are in conflict with those of your preschool program. What are possible outcomes for this conflict situation?

1. The difference may not be resolved because neither program nor family will change their positions even though they know about the other's perspective. This is the least desirable outcome. You cannot understand the family's position and will not change yours. The family reacts in a similar fashion. This standoff inhibits communication and prevents the development of a collaborative relationship between program and family. Further, Lisa is placed in the middle of the conflict between the expectations of her family and those of the preschool program. She may feel

anxious about participating in activities that she knows her family does not endorse; she also may sense disapproval from the adults in the program and encounter rejection from the other children.

2. The differences may disappear if the program changes to accommodate the family's perspective. You give in to the family's position and decide to focus on more early literacy strategies (as described in Chapter 6). The program changes the curriculum focus from an emphasis on outdoor and active play to a Montessori-type curriculum that emphasizes problem-solving using manipulative, self-correcting materials, practical life activities in self-help, and language development.

3. The difference may disappear if the family changes to accommodate the program's perspective. Influenced by your explanation of developmentally appropriate practice, the family decides they want Lisa to "fit in" with the expectations of the preschool, so they buy some "play clothes" for her to wear and agree that she can participate in active play activities at school.

4. The differences may disappear if both sides compromise and view each other's perspective. This is the optimal or most desirable outcome. You and the family understand and appreciate each other's point of view. The family agrees that Lisa can wear shorts under her dress when playing outside and a paint smock during the arts and crafts lesson. You agree to provide additional indoor activities such as puzzles and books, and to make sure Lisa is cleaned up at the end of the day.

Ask yourself . . .
- *Has there been a situation where your early childhood practice or suggestion created a conflict with a family?*
  —What was the specific situation, practice, or suggestion?
  —How did you discover there was a conflict between your program practice and the family's values and priorities?
  —How did the family respond?
  —What did you do?
  —What was the outcome? Was the conflict resolved? If so, how?
  —What did you learn from this experience?
  —What would you do differently next time?

❖ BUILDING A RELATIONSHIP WITH FAMILIES

As illustrated in Lisa's situation, it is most important to find out about the family's concerns, goals, and expectations for their child, and be aware of the possible mismatch with the families your program serves. At the same time, families should know the program goals and expectations. In our earlier example, Jennifer Gregg was surprised and shocked to learn from her supervisor that Mei-Mei's parents were unhappy with the preschool program. They nodded when she explained the curriculum and the importance of the daily painting activity for the children's creative expression and self-esteem but Jennifer did not realize that the Kwans were indicating they heard what she said but did not agree with the curriculum.

Simple but meaningful practices facilitate communication with a family and develop a collaborative relationship. The following points discuss ways to help you build a relationship with the children and families in your program.

- Find out who makes decisions in the family, who you should invite to meetings, who you should speak to about program activities and issues related to the child, and who you should invite to participate in program activities.
- Find out how to address the parents and other adult family members in respectful ways. In some cultures; for example, African American adults should be addressed formally, such as Mr. Jones or Miss Barrett. Use of first names are considered too informal and disrespectful. In other cultures, it may be acceptable to call a person by the family or social relationship instead of by a given name, for example, "Lisa's mother."
- In a number of Asian cultures (Korean, Cambodian, Chinese, Hmong, and Vietnamese), husbands and wives have different surnames because the women keep their family names (Dresser, 1996), for example, Kim Yeo Suk married Ho Tuan Park. Family names or surnames place first, so the correct form of address is Mrs. Kim and Mr. Ho. Mexican women keep their maiden names as

well and add the husband's name after the word de (of); for example, Maria Selva becomes Maria Selva de Lopez when she marries Fernando Lopez. Their children have their given name, father's family name, and mother's family name (Dresser, 1996), for example, Eriberto Lopez Selva. As you can see, these differences from the first and last name conventions in the United States result in confusion about surnames and in how to address children and families from different cultural backgrounds. When in doubt, ask family members how they prefer to be addressed and how to pronounce their names.

- When working with a family who speaks a language different from your own, work with an interpreter knowledgeable about the family's culture as well. Ideally, the interpreter also is familiar with your early childhood program and the relevant terms. In reality, you may have to orient the interpreter to program goals and explain terminology. With all families, you should use clear and simple language, not professional jargon (Chen, Chan, & Brekken, 2000). However, when you use an interpreter, precise, easily understood language is even more important. Think about how you would explain "developmentally appropriate practice" or "transition to the next age group." These are not common concepts for the average English speaking family, much less for families who do not speak English. Learn some greetings and common phrases in the family's language. The family will appreciate your interest and attempts at communication. Use concrete examples such as objects, pictures, videos, and other props to demonstrate concepts and other information that you want to share with the family.

- Ask the family about what they expect and would like for their child in your program. Listen carefully to what they say and build on their priorities when describing what the program provides. In many cultures, you are viewed as the expert who is responsible for their children's education, and parents would not think of offering an opinion about the program or their children's participation. When dealing with these families, obtaining their perspectives and priorities for their children requires time, effort, and skillful communication.

Ask yourself . . .
- *What strategies should you use to facilitate communication with families from diverse backgrounds?*
- *How do you gather information from families?*
- *How do you select and train interpreters?*
- *How do you provide information to families?*
- *What strategies do you use to make sure that families receive accurate information?*
- *How do you prepare for a meeting with families whose language you do not speak?*
- *How do you plan for the meeting with the interpreter?*
- *What strategies do you use to determine what you say is interpreted accurately and understood by the family?*

❖ SUMMARY

This chapter challenges you to think in some detail about the ways in which your early childhood program addresses the needs of culturally diverse children and their families. The recent NAEYC best practices guidelines provide a new commitment to inclusive early childhood education. This requires a conscientious consideration of values and philosophy, as well as specific strategies and day-to-day practices. The following chapters in this book provide you with specific information regarding how language and culture influence the behavior and development of young children. We hope these chapters will provide some of the information and skills necessary to implement a culturally rich early childhood program. We also hope it will motivate you to embark on a lifelong journey of developing "cross cultural competence."

❖ REFERENCES

Bowman, B. T., & Stott, F. M. (1994). Understanding development in a cultural context: The challenge for teachers. In B. L. Mallory & R. S. New (eds.). *Diversity & developmentally appropriate practices. Challenges of early childhood education* (pp.119–133). New York: Teachers College Press.

Bredekamp, S., & Copple, C. (Eds.). (1997). *Developmentally appropriate practices in early childhood programs*. (Revised edition). Washington, DC: NAEYC.

Carlson, V. J., & Harwood, R. L. (2000). Understanding and negotiating cultural differences concerning early developmental competence. *Zero to Three, 20*(3), 19–24.

Chang, H. N. L., Muckelroy, A., & Pulido-Tobiassen, D. (1996). *Looking in, looking out. Redefining child care and early education in a diverse society*. San Francisco: Tomorrow.

Chen, D., Chan, S., & Brekken, L. (2000). *Conversations for three. Communicating through interpreters*. [Video and booklet.] Baltimore: Paul H. Brookes Publishing.

Day, D. E. (1983). *Early childhood education*. Palo Alto, CA: Scott, Foresman and Company.

Derman-Sparks, L., & the A.B.C. Task Force. (1989). *Anti-bias curriculum: Tools for empowering young children*. Washington, DC: NAEYC.

Dresser, N. (1996). *Multicultural manners. New rules of etiquette for a changing society*. New York: John Wiley.

Gollnick, D. M., & Chinn, P. C. (1994). *Multicultural education in a pluralistic society* (4th ed.). Columbus, OH: Macmillan.

Gonzalez-Mena, J. (1992). Taking a culturally sensitive approach in infant-toddler programs. *Young Children, 47*(2), 4–9.

Gonzalez-Mena, J. (1993). *Multicultural issues in child care*. Mountain View, CA: Mayfield Publishing.

Green, J. W. (1982). *Cultural awareness in the human services*. Englewood Cliffs, NJ: Prentice-Hall.

Kendall, F. E. (1983). *Diversity in the classroom: A multicultural approach to the education of young children*. New York: Teachers College Press.

Kostelnik, M. J. (1992). Myths associated with developmentally appropriate programs. *Young Children, 47*(4), 17–23.

Lacayo, R. (April 14, 1997). The kids are all right. Day care - mostly harmless sometimes helpful and less important than home. *Time*, 75.

Loden, M., & Rosener, J. (1991). *Workforce America!* Burr Ridge, IL: Business One Irwin.

Ludlow, B. L., & Berkeley, T. R. (1994). Expanding the perceptions of developmentally appropriate practice: Changing theoretical perspectives. In B. L. Mallory & R. S. New (eds.). *Diversity & developmentally appropriate practices. Challenges of early childhood education* (pp. 107–118). New York: Teachers College Press.

Lynch, E. W., & Hanson, M. J. (1998). *Developing cross-cultural competence. A guide for working with young children and their families* (2d ed.). Baltimore: Paul H. Brookes Publishing.

Mallory, B. L., & New, R. S. (Eds.). (1994). *Diversity and developmentally appropriate practices: Challenges of early childhood education*. New York: Teachers College Press.

National Academy of Early Childhood Programs. (1984). Accreditation criteria and procedures of the National Academy of Early Childhood Programs. Washington, DC: National Association for the Education of Young Children.

National Association for the Education of Young Children. (1991). Accreditation criteria and procedures of the National Academy of Early Childhood Programs (rev. ed.). Washington, DC: National Association for the Education of Young Children.

NAEYC (1994). NAEYC Position Statement: A conceptual framework for early childhood professional development. *Young Children, 49*(3), 68–77.

National Association for the Education of Young Children. (1996). NAEYC Position Statement: Responding to linguistic and cultural diversity. Recommendations for effective early childhood education. *Young Children, 51*(4), 4–12.

Phillips, C. B. (1994). The movement of African-American children through sociocultural contexts: A case of conflict resolution. In B. L. Mallory & R. S. New (eds.). *Diversity & developmentally appropriate practices. Challenges of early childhood education* (pp.137–154). New York: Teachers College Press.

Sameroff, A. J., & Chandler, M. (1975). Reproductive risk and the continuum of caregiving casualty. In F. Horowitz, M. Hetherington, S. Scarr-Salapatek, & G. Seigel (eds.). *Review of child development research* (Vol. 4, pp. 187–245). Chicago: University of Chicago Press.

Schulze, P. A., Harwood, R. L., Goebel, M. J., & Schubert, A. M. (1999). Cultural influences on mothers' developmental expectations for their children. Poster presented at the Biennial meeting of the Society for Research in Child Development. Albuquerque, NM.

Turnbull, A. P., & Turnbull, H. R. (1996). *Families, professionals, and exceptionality. A special partnership* (3rd ed.). Upper Saddle River, NJ: Merrill.

Wong Fillmore, L. (1991). When learning a second language means losing the first. *Early Childhood Research Quarterly, 6,* 323–346.

Wright, R. (April 14, 1997). Why Johnny can't sleep. *Time,* 74–75.

York, S. (1991). *Roots & wings. Affirming culture in early childhood programs.* St. Paul, MN: Redleaf Press.

❖ CHAPTER 3

Understanding Cultural Differences in Family Child-Rearing Practices

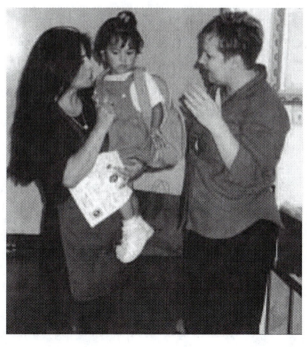

It is extremely important for early childhood professionals to understand that, with few exceptions, all parents want their children to be happy, healthy and successful. Parents do their best within the context of their own values and beliefs, and within the constraints of their resources. Norton (1990) states that "Human beings raise their children to fit into the society they know. Child rearing practices reflect what parents know about life in their community, what they believe will be useful, and what they recognize as realistic aspirations for their children" (p. 3).

Attitudes and beliefs about what is best for children and specific child-rearing practices vary in many ways according to complex influences. Some of these influences include, but are not limited to:

- the infant or child's temperament and behavior;
- the child's parent's own previous role models for parenting;
- beliefs about parents' roles;
- beliefs about how children learn and the nature of child development;
- religious beliefs;
- availability of resources and environmental constraints;
- family structure and organization; and
- degree of isolation from other cultures and/or communities.

This list of influences reflects the material resources as well as the cultural factors manifested in the day-to-day activities of families. Furthermore, these influences are constantly changing. Families are dynamic rather than static entities. They are always changing and must continuously adapt to the material and cultural influences around them. This is the essence of "ecocultural niche theory" described by Gallimore, Weisner, Kaufman, and Bernheimer (1989). This theory helps provide a framework for our appreciation of the complex and dynamic nature of families.

The purpose of this chapter is to provide you, the early childhood professional, with an understanding of the many influences on family child-rearing values and behavior, and specifically of the dimensions along which families vary as they strive toward one universal goal: the healthy growth and well-being of their children.

This chapter also describes the biases and tendencies of middle-class mainstream society's assumptions about appropriate child-rearing practices and provides many examples of how these may differ from other cultures and communities (see Deloache & Gottlieb, 2000).

❖ ENVIRONMENTAL/SOCIOECONOMIC INFLUENCES

Physical survival is obviously a universal goal of all families. Circumstances such as poverty, crime, or war, which significantly threaten that survival, exert powerful influences on family structure and child-rearing beliefs and practices. Ogbu (1974) discusses certain realities of African American families living in inner city ghettos. Economic hardship and the violence of daily life force mothers to teach their children survival skills. He describes these mothers as nurturing during infancy, but less nurturing and inflicting more physical punishment as children become older. This reflects the parents' efforts to avoid spoiling the child. He further suggests that such early environments produce children who are self-reliant, manipulative, mistrustful of authority figures, and who can fight back and defend themselves. He also suggests that years of predominantly peer group association rather than adult-child interactions better enable them to adapt to the environment of the street culture

Hale-Benson (1986) reports a study of African American grandmothers' attitudes toward child rearing. One interesting difference between the attitudes of black and white grandmothers was related to the importance of learning to defend oneself by fighting back. White grandmothers generally did not encourage children to fight back whereas black grandmothers often expressed the feeling that children should be punished for *not* fighting back to defend themselves. Viewed within the context of inner city life, being able to defend oneself is indeed an important survival skill.

Inner city parents often have great fear of not being able to protect their children from the many dangers of their neighborhoods. As a result, they may appear overprotective or overcontrolling (Franklin & Boyd-Franklin, 1985).

The Effects of Scarce Resources

One of the most obvious environmental influences is the availability of resources. For example, poverty and tradition often encourage the development of family structures that include extended family members, and sometimes close family friends, within the same residence. Such arrangements often result in multiple and sometimes inconsistent caregivers. These homes are viewed as chaotic by middle-class standards, and fine-tuned responses to young children's cues may be difficult to define. As an early childhood professional, you may tend to view such environments as problematic. Yet it is an important adaptation to the reality of poverty. Parents cannot afford to pay for child care and reliable child-care programs may not even exist. Mothers must work to meet families' basic needs and, therefore, multiple caregivers and immediate access to extended family members are adaptations important to children's survival.

Examples of the influence of poverty on child-rearing practices are endless. The provision of appropriate toys and learning materials, such as books and crayons, and access to experiences such as movies, fairs, the zoo, concerts, and vacations require financial resources. Transportation is also a limited resource. Frequent diaper changes to keep babies dry necessitates the money to buy diapers. Encouraging infants to develop self-feeding skills results in wasting food that is spilled, thrown on the floor, or ends up in the child's hair. Poor families cannot afford such waste, regardless of how developmentally appropriate the professionals considers it to be.

A study reported by Zussman (1978) clearly demonstrates the influence of stress on child-rearing behavior. An experiment was conducted with middle-class parents and their young children. Parents and their children were divided into two groups and placed in a playroom with their children. The first group simply watched and assisted their children. The second group of parents were given a moderately difficult paper-and-pencil problem to solve while keeping an eye on their children. The results of the study showed that even this mild stressor significantly influenced how parents interacted with their children. Parents who tried to do the paper-and-pencil task were less responsive and more controlling. Families living in poverty often experience disproportionate amounts of stress related to their fear of violence and the difficulty of coping with limited resources. These conditions often are present in low income neighborhoods, particularly in urban housing projects.

The following true story captures some of the realities as well as successful strategies for working with families living in poverty.

> A low-income, recently immigrated family enrolled their two-year-old child in an early intervention program. The program began at 9:00 each morning. The child consistently was too sleepy to participate in the program. The staff discussed this with the mother and learned that there were two families living in a two-room apartment. The adults in the household spent the evening watching television or talking until the wee hours of the morning. Adults, as well as children, went to sleep when they were tired. This is not an unusual practice among nonmainstream families. The two-year-old often was awake until two or three in the morning, but had to awaken at 7:00 a.m. to take the bus with his mother to the program. A visit to the family's apartment revealed they did not own a crib. The early intervention teacher did not think to ask if there was a bed for the child. After the visit, the teacher tactfully commented that if the family felt a crib for the baby might enable him to go to sleep earlier, she would be happy to obtain one for them. Two or three weeks later, the mother asked how she might obtain a crib. It was quickly arranged and the family placed the crib in a corner of the living room. The mother put the baby to bed earlier each night. The baby loved the crib and fell asleep quickly despite the background noises. He was markedly more rested and alert when he came to the center.

The Value of Obedience

Levine's cross-cultural studies (1974) suggest that in more affluent populations, independence and autonomy are valued over obedience whereas families with scarce resources often place a higher value on obedience. Again, this has survival value for poor families. According to Kohn (1977), child-rearing attitudes and values often relate to the kind of work the father does. Kohn cautions against making value judgments about the child-rearing practices of the working class and of poor families. For example, working class occupations often demand obedience and punctuality under supervision; middle-class occupations may be more complex and require more self-direction without supervision. Therefore, the child-rearing practices of working class families may be realistic and adaptive for *their* children's future needs. Another important factor related to societal influences on child-rearing beliefs and practices is the degree of isolation from other communities and cultures. According to Norton (1990), families living in the urban isolation of the inner city often are separated from important institutions and resources and cannot teach their children the "rules and tools" necessary for success in the mainstream (p. 3). The more isolated the family is from other cultural influences, the more discrepant their behaviors from mainstream behaviors.

❖ THE INFLUENCE OF RACISM

Closely related to the threats to one's physical survival found in poverty and violence are the threats to one's sense of self and one's livelihood which result from racism. While all minorities experience racism to some extent, none is so profound in the United States as the discrimination experienced by African Americans. This fundamental bias is part of the very fabric of our society. Despite historic and contemporary efforts to overcome bias, racism continues to be a basic and usually dominant force in the daily lives of African Americans.

Racial identity plays a major role in the child-rearing practices of African Americans. According to a study by Peters (1985), the major challenge of child rearing perceived by African American parents is to prepare their children to cope and survive in a racist society. They often teach their children that life will not be fair to them. They emphasize the value of education as a means of fighting racial barriers and they strongly emphasize the importance of pride and self-esteem.

Middle-class professionals sometimes view African Americans as paranoid and defensive. Yet the reality of racism cannot be denied. The attitudes of African American families toward professionals and the values these parents instill in their children can be understood only within the historical and contemporary context of racial discrimination in the United States.

The writing of Boykin and Toms (1985) describes the "triple quandary" faced by African Americans, the struggle to reconcile three very different cultural influences in their lives: mainstream United States culture, the culture of an oppressed minority, and African American culture which has its roots in the values and traditions of West Africa. Mann (2000) discusses this quandary in terms of the multiple tasks of parenting, and the need to balance three contexts:

1. the majority context, which values competition and individual achievement;
2. the minority context, which requires parents teach coping strategies to deal with discrimination and negative social experiences; and
3. the cultural context, which values historical traditions such as spirituality and communalism.

Parents know this challenge, both for themselves and for their children, is even more difficult because of the lack of congruence among these influences.

Although this dilemma of reconciling disparate influences and characteristics into an integrated self-image is difficult for African Americans in particular, it is a problem for all minority families. As an early childhood professional, you must recognize this important difference between mainstream and nonmainstream families. By definition, mainstream families have goals, values, and child-rearing practices congruent with the majority culture and which, therefore, prepare their children to be successful in that culture. Mainstream families do not have to face the challenge of developing in their children an integrated sense of self that must somehow reconcile disparate cultural influences.

Mainstream professionals may view parents' efforts to teach their children about racism as a practice that fosters paranoia. However, a testament to the effectiveness of this child-rearing practice is found in the research literature on self-esteem in African American children. Despite undeniably negative media messages and daily experiences, African American children do not have lower self-esteem than other cultural groups (Taylor, 1994; Powell, 1985). For many children, the strength of the family provides an important buffer against pervasive racism (Hale, 1991; Phillips, 1994).

❖ THE INFLUENCE OF RELIGION

Religion often plays a major role in families' attitudes toward child rearing and in child-rearing practices. The United States is a country of religious pluralism. There are hundreds of recognized religions in the country, and an unknown number of informal religious groups and cults. Religions vary in the extent to which they influence the daily lives of their members. While nine out of ten Americans indicate their religious beliefs are very important or fairly important to them (Gallup Report, 1989), only half attend church on a regular basis. Some families are not influenced by their religion whereas the religious beliefs of others exert a major influence on their daily behaviors, their interactions with others, and on their subjective experience, and their interpretation of life events.

Weisner, Beizer, and Stolze (1991) studied the influence of religion on families of children with developmental delays. Their findings suggested that religion plays an an important role in how parents describe and interpret situations, and that religion is particularly powerful as a way of explaining their children's disabilities. The study also found that religious families were more focused on the family and on parents' roles as teachers and nurturers. They also were more likely to participate in social activities than were nonreligious families. The study did not find, however, that religious families received more overall support (material and interpersonal).

Many Western religions are congruent with the major values of the dominant culture. They tend to emphasize individual control and self-responsibility. Other religions foster a more passive view, stating that all events are explained by supernatural forces. These different views influence how families raise their children.

Many examples are offered relating to the influence of religion on child rearing. One of the most familiar early Christian traditions is "Spare the rod; spoil the child." This suggests that children must be aggressively disciplined for inappropriate behavior, and that overindulgence of children is undesirable. This is an important religious belief within many African American communities that results in a reliance on physical punishment as the primary disciplinary strategy (Franklin & Boyd-Franklin, (1985). In many Asian families, when a child brings serious shame on himself and his family, use of physical punishment is considered appropriate (Chan, 1998).

Many religions, such as Christianity and Judaism, and the philosophy of Confucianism, place a strong emphasis on the importance of *teaching*. For example, a well-known Christian Bible verse says, "And teach a child in the way he should go." In both Confucian and Bhuddist traditions, one of the most important responsibilities of parents is teaching their children how to behave properly and live lives that honor the family and their ancestors.

The Role of Religion in Explaining Disability

Religion plays an especially important role in how families view health and disability. For example, the

Church of the Latter Day Saints (Mormons) believe
that a child with a disability preexisted as a perfect
being, and will go on to the Celestial Kingdom as that
perfect being. The time spent on earth with a disability
is a short time compared to eternity. This view facilitates the family's acceptance of the child. In Jewish tradition, there is no theological explanation for a child's
disability. It just happens; it is not an act of God.
Roman Catholic theology supports the contention that
redemption is a continual process. Since mankind continues to sin, suffering continues to exist to redeem
everyone for their sins. Therefore, while the child and
parents themselves are guiltless, the disabled child
serves as a "sacrificial lamb" for all so that everyone's
sins can be forgiven.

In many cultures, there is a belief that if a child is
born with a disability or has serious illness, God is
punishing the family for some wrongdoing. Usually it
is the mother's behavior that brought about the punishment. This is a very strong belief that continues
even through generations of acculturation. For example, a good friend of the author is from a Mexican,
Catholic background. Despite the fact that she is a
highly educated, middle-class professional, when her
son was born with a disability, she believed it was her
punishment from God for having watched a porno-
graphic film!

Sometimes the belief that the child's condition is
an act of God makes it very difficult for families to seek
help from professionals. Parents believe that trying to
"fix" or intervene in any way with the child's disability
is questioning God's authority. Families are inclined to
accept the child as is, and to bear the burden of the
child's disability as appropriate punishment for past
sins. Challenging God's authority is the ultimate sin.

It is easy to see how parents whose religion influences them in this way feel conflicted about early education and intervention for their child. "The system"
—mainstream health care and social services in the
United States—expect them to seek out services aggressively and to follow through on the suggestions of various health and education professionals such as a
physician's recommendations about medications or
surgery, a physical therapist's instructions about exer-
cises to improve motor control, a speech pathologist's

suggestions about talking in certain ways to the child, or the teacher's request that the parent attend parent training sessions on a regular basis to learn how to carry over the activities of an intervention program. Parents are well aware that "the system" believes these are important things to do. They also may feel that mainstream professionals believe if parents do not participate in these activities, they are inadequate and unconcerned. At the same time, parents may have strong "gut-level" emotions that tell them such interventions are in some way wrong.

In addition, some families may feel shame because of a child with a disability. Asian parents who view their child's disability as retribution for their wrongdoing may be hesitant to place their child in a special program where all the world sees the evidence of their behavior.

The emotional conflict that results from these opposing influences of religious beliefs and societal expectations is obvious. This conflict often creates ambivalence toward the intervention program. This ambivalence, in turn, often manifests itself in inconsistent participation in programs. One teacher in an early intervention program that served a multiethnic population frequently expressed frustration that several families only attended the center about half the time, and sometimes were not home when the teacher arrived for home visits. When the parents interacted with the teacher, they were always positive about their intentions to follow through on the child's programming and attend more regularly. Despite the fact that interpreters were used consistently to make sure communication was clear and that any concerns could be freely expressed, the parents never expressed concern or discomfort with any of the activities or procedures. What is difficult for mainstream professionals to realize is that probably these parents are not fully conscious of their own ambivalence and conflict. Parents themselves may not understand why it is so difficult to follow through or to enthusiastically participate in their young child's intervention and therapies. It is extremely important that you avoid making these parents feel guilty for not participating as consistently as you would like. This does not mean that you do not explain the value of repetition and consistency in helping children learn. It simply means that you avoid the implication that parents are "bad" and that they are willfully harming their child by not following through or attending the program regularly. Adding guilt to their already existing unease about the appropriateness of trying to change their child's condition only *decreases* the likelihood that they will continue to participate at any level in the program.

In some families while there may be a religious belief that the disability is God's will, it is not seen as a punishment. This religious belief is a significant source of support. Sometimes the child is seen as "God's gift", or as a focal point to bring the family closer together. For these families, spirituality offers important emotional support for dealing with the child's disability or health problem. For example, in many Native American tribes, all children, including children with disabilities, are accepted for what they are. It should be noted, however, there also may be a tendency to avoid early education and intervention. The nature of young children is viewed as relatively impervious to efforts by adults to change it.

Influence of Religion on Gender Roles

An area of marked difference between mainstream and nonmainstream cultures is in the area of gender roles and expectations. Parents often have distinctly different expectations and ways of interacting with boys and girls, usually beginning in infancy. These values and practices are related, in part, to religious influences. In most religions—the Roman Catholic Church, the Church of Latter Day Saints, and even in some protestant churches—women are barred from assuming leadership positions simply because they are female. According to Van Leeuwen (1990), many biblical scholars interpret the Bible to say that God gave man, through Adam (Genesis 1:26-27), dominion over Eve, and therefore over all women. Other scholars use the same scriptures and interpret them to mean that God gave Adam and Eve (man and woman) dominion over every other living creature. In those families whose religion suggests that women are of lower status, masculine and feminine roles are usually clearly defined, and young children are taught from the beginning to assume these roles. This topic is discussed in greater length in Chapter 4, Cultural Influences on Young Children's Social Skills and Behaviors.

❖ FAMILY STRUCTURE AND MULTIPLE CAREGIVERS

For various reasons (including economic necessity, discussed earlier), family structures and the roles of caregivers often are different in nonmainstream culture families. The middle-class preference for relatively small nuclear families consisting of mother, father (or a single mother), and two or three children, is unusual when compared with families from most other non-European backgrounds. Most cultures include maternal or paternal grandparents in the family structure, and even aunts, uncles, cousins, and close family friends. By comparison, the small nuclear family is relatively isolated. Nonmainstream families view such family structures as lacking adequate social support for nurturing and caretaking young children. The reliance of mainstream families on child care provided *outside* the home by relative strangers is viewed as inappropriate.

On the other hand, you, as an early childhood professional, may view large, extended, multigenerational families as chaotic. As mentioned earlier in this chapter, you may be concerned about consistency in child rearing because there are multiple caretakers. It is important to realize, however, that only a generation or two ago, this was the norm in many mainstream families in the United States. Particularly in farm families living in rural America, families with seven or eight children were not unusual. It was also common for a widowed grandparent to live with the family. Although not formally ascribed as in some cultural groups, older siblings often took responsibility for younger children. Since mothers were typically full-time homemakers, child care outside the home was uncommon; children rarely experienced peer groups or caregivers outside the home until formal schooling began at age five or six. Children raised in this environment were not considered as suffering from chaotic and/or inconsistent child rearing; nor were they considered socially deprived.

❖ INFLUENCE OF "COLLECTIVIST" VIEWS ON CHILD-REARING PRACTICES

Earlier in this text we discussed the predominance of "collectivist" versus "individualistic" views of the world. Collectivism has important influences on the ways people raise children. In collectivist families, particularly in Asian cultures influenced by Confucian values, a keynote of family existence is harmony and the maintenance of social order (Chinn & Wong, 1992; Chan, 1998). In many Asian cultures, one of the most important values taught to children is the principle of "filial piety": honoring, respecting, and obeying ones parents. Children must not bring shame or loss of face to their parents. This expectation lasts forever and extends past the parents' death, particularly through the Bhuddist practice of ancestor worship and respect (Te, 1989).

In order to maintain order and harmony, the roles and ranks of individual family members are ascribed and delineated. Typically, the father is the ultimate authority and extends not only to the children but also to the wife. In Vietnamese families, however, the wife is responsible for the children and the home, and has the "power of the purse" (Te, 1989). The children actually view the father and mother as having equal authority.) The roles and responsibilities of each of the children usually is determined by age and gender, the oldest males having the greatest responsibility.

Such formally established hierarchies, where obedience and respect are the key attributes learned by children, have a profound influence on child rearing. We already mentioned the use of corporal punishment in instances where children's behavior is considered particularly shameful or disrespectful. The use of "shaming" is a common practice in many Asian families (Chinn & Wong, 1992; Harry, 1992). Children learn that their behavior not only disgraces themselves but also, and even worse, disgraces the family and all their ancestors.

In many Asian families, infants and toddlers are not usually disciplined. An indulgent and nurturing environment is created for very young children. As children enter the preschool years, however, expectations for them to behave properly and assume greater family responsibility increase significantly, and sometimes abruptly.

Another area of great influence on the principle of respect for rank and authority of family members is on parent-child communication patterns. Chapter 5, Cultural Influences on Communication Skills and Styles, describes many specific differences in the ways parents use language when talking to young children. Many of these differences relate to the hierarchical structure of families. In the United States, the family interaction patterns are often democratic. Mainstream American culture places a very strong value on verbal assertiveness and competence. In many mainstream families, children even have the right to challenge the directives and decisions of adults. There is a belief that even young children should be allowed to explain and defend themselves, ask questions, and carry on conversations with adults. Furthermore, children must learn to engage in these communicative behaviors with competence, and it is a goal of parent-child interactions to facilitate the development of these skills. These skills, in turn, translate into the very skills important to school success and to literacy achievement.

In many—if not most—nonmainstream cultures, verbal behaviors such as rationalizing, asking questions, and conversing with adults are considered inappropriate. In many families, children *listen* while adults or older siblings *speak*. In some cultures, adults rarely talk to very young children. Adults do not talk to an infant or very young child until the child has learned to talk (Heath, 1983). Compare this with the typical United States attitude that children learn to talk best because of adults' responsive interactions with them. This presents a serious values mis-match. Early childhood education programs, as well as early intervention programs, strongly value activities that help children develop verbal abilities. Often, the kinds of activities modeled in these programs, such as adults expanding on children's utterances and following children's leads in conversations, are completely foreign to some parents. It requires learning a new skill—a new way of interacting with their children—that is quite contrary to the norms of their culture.

❖ THE INFLUENCE OF BELIEFS ABOUT THE NATURE OF CHILDHOOD AND HOW CHILDREN LEARN

Mainstream American families view children as initially helpless. Since mainstream culture places high value on independence and self-reliance, a major child-rearing agenda is to help children achieve greater and greater independence. Parents are aware of developmental milestones and take pride when their child achieves these milestones at an earlier than expected age. Self-help skills such as walking, dressing, feeding, and talking are considered particularly important reflections of a child's increasing independence. Latino and African American families also value independence, but in somewhat different ways (Westby, 1985). While there is not so much emphasis on verbal precocity, African American and Latino families encourage physical independence, and the ability of children to defend themselves. According to Briggs (1984), Latino children, especially males, are taught to defend the "Dignidad de la persona." African American families are particularly concerned with avoiding overindulgence of children so they do not become "spoiled" (Field & Widmayer, 1981).

Many Asian families, however, do *not* encourage independence (reflecting the value of collectivism). They see infants and young children as initially willful and self-centered. These characteristics are discouraged. Early child rearing in many Asian families encourages contentedness in infants, and often anticipates infants' needs so they do not need to initiate to make their needs known. This thought process is the opposite of those cultures which purposely create the need to initiate so that children learn to communicate wants and needs.

Another area where you, as an early childhood professional, will find a difference in families' views of young children is in relation to the communicative values of infant behaviors. Middle-class mainstream families respond to even the simplest infant behavior as though it is intentionally communicative. For example, the infant sighs or gurgles and the adult immediately responds by saying something like "What did you say?" or "Oh you're happy aren't you!" At the other end of this continuum are the Appalachian black families described in a study by Heath (1983). In this community, infant vocalizations were not considered communicative and were not responded to as such. Adults did not typically talk to young children until the children were able to use words. Similarly, Latino women do not consider their young infants' communications as intentional until around 14 months of age (Eisenberg, 1982).

A third area in which significant differences exist in parents' views of how children learn is related to their own roles as *teachers* of their children. Most cultures believe parents have some role in teaching their children. The differences lie in *what* is taught and *how* it is taught (Quinn, 1995).

Mainstream middle-class families in the United States are concerned particularly with teaching their children to talk and to achieve other important developmental milestones. They also believe it is important to teach certain social behaviors, such as saying "please" and "thank you," and sharing with others. But this is not generally considered their primary teaching role. In African American families, parents often see their primary teaching role as enabling their children to cope with racism. Compliance is also an important goal in African American families; for example, teaching the child to "mind." In poverty areas, low socioeconomic status (SES) families often must prioritize teaching children to survive in hostile environments. In many Asian families, the primary goal is teaching children to behave properly (Luangpraseut, 1989; Te, 1989), to obey their elders, and to honor the family and ancestors through achievements such as academic success (Chinn & Wong, 1992).

Families also have very different beliefs about *how* children learn, and what teaching strategies are most effective. Mainstream Euro-American and European families emphasize "social mediation of the environment" (Anastasiow, 1986),as espoused in the theories of Bruner (1982), Vygotsky(1978), and Feuerstein, et al. (1980). In essence, this approach states that adults must be responsive to children's interests and to their communicative attempts by using language as well as physical assistance to help the child expand his or her understanding of the world, advance to the next level of development, and refine language and reasoning skills. This approach is *responsive* and highly *interactive*. It also values *play* as an important context in which to teach children. When we examine the history of early childhood education in the United States, as well as the kindergarten movement in Europe, these themes are pervasive.

Perhaps another important characteristic of middle-class approaches to child rearing in the United States is a greater reliance on "experts" and research in such fields as developmental psychology as opposed to religious doctrine or family tradition. As a result, the specifics of our child-rearing practices are constantly changing as the experts' theories change. Unfortunately, this often creates confusion about the "best" way to raise children, especially for younger parents. Parents may lack self-confidence in their parenting abilities. They may seek assistance from parenting classes, books and magazines, friends, and professionals.

Many families from nonmainstream backgrounds may place relatively greater emphasis on *direct instruction* and learning through *imitation*. A common language teaching strategy used in Latino homes is a triadic interaction in which the parent instructs the child to say something to someone else (Eisenberg, 1982). Parents and older siblings teach younger children to make tortillas or work in a garden by physically demonstrating the behavior and asking the child to imitate.

In other cultures, there is a belief that children learn, not through direct instruction or responsive interaction, but simply by being in the company of adults and *observing*. For example, in many African American communities (Heath, 1983), Native American communities, and in Western Samoa (Ochs, 1982), children are expected to learn primarily through observation. They are not segregated from adult social interaction and have many opportunities to observe language and social customs. The language learning process is quite different for these children when compared to mainstream children. It is as if these children must "break the code" on their own. Both Heath and Ochs report that children in these communities begin to use language by spontaneously imitating the final words of sentences and words that are highly stressed, such as expletives (for example, "darn!") In Laotian culture, according to Luang-praseut (1989), adults purposely *avoid* giving direct instruction to children. Yet children learning appropriate social behavior is very important. The primary method of teaching is through observation.

In many Asian families, an important teaching strategy is through adults' use of language to exhort and teach appropriate behaviors, and to explain important traditions and principles. The child's role is to listen respectfully while the adult explains. In traditional Asian families, there is relatively little interaction between parents and children, especially between fathers and children. Communication is generally one way: "The parent speaks; the child listens" (Chan, 1998, p. 302).

❖ PROFILES OF CHARACTERISTIC CHILD-REARING PRACTICES IN FIVE CULTURAL GROUPS: MAINSTREAM AMERICAN MIDDLE-CLASS; TRADITIONAL ASIAN; AFRICAN AMERICAN; LATINO; AND NATIVE AMERICAN

As stressed throughout this text, there are many dangers associated with the attempt to make generalizations about the characteristics of any particular group. When we use an ecocultural approach to understanding families' child-rearing practices, we realize that what and how parents teach their children is dependent on many factors, including the influences discussed so far in this chapter.

Despite this important caveat, there *are* certain child-rearing practices likely to be characteristic of a particular group. Again, depending on the degree of a family's acculturation to mainstream American culture, and the influence of other factors such as economic status and religion, the profiles described here may or may not be characteristic of any individual family. It is important for the early childhood professional to realize it is entirely possible for a particular Asian family in your program to have *nothing* in common with the "typical child-rearing practices of families with Asian roots" we present here.

Typical Child-rearing Practices of Mainstream Middle-Class American Families

Perhaps the most important notion for you to come to terms with regarding middle-class child rearing in the United States is how different it is from the countries of origin of most families who immigrate here. Furthermore, these child-rearing practices also may also be quite different from those of American families living in poor urban or poor rural environments.

Mainstream Middle-class America

"Democratic" Parenting Style. Perhaps as a reflection of mainstream culture's value of democratic principles, middle-class families in the United States tend to be relatively nonauthoritarian when compared to most other cultures. This parenting style allows for much reciprocal interaction which begins at birth. Children are encouraged to ask questions of adults and to give explanations. Children's input to settling family disputes often is accepted and valued. Children's wishes are granted if they present compelling arguments or if they are persistent in their requests. The early roots of this pattern is seen in the familiar grocery store scenario: as mother pushes the cart through the aisles, her young child points and whines as the

cart passes the cookies and candy. These communications are often effective in convincing mother to make unintended purchases. Such compliance is viewed as grossly overindulgent and inappropriate by many non-mainstream mothers. Yet this pattern reflects the theme of responsivity to infant/child cues so pervasive in middle-class families.

Democratic, "egalitarian" approaches to child rearing also produce discipline patterns different from non-mainstream families. For example, in the United States today, authoritarian parenting styles are viewed as inappropriate by most mainstream individuals (Harry, 1992). The use of corporal punishment—once an almost universally accepted discipline strategy in the United States—now is considered unacceptable by many mainstream families and is even illegal if excessive.

Responsivity to Child Communicative Cues. A tendency toward responsivity and "following the child's lead" also is reflected in patterns of communicative interaction. Mainstream parents talk to their children far more than most other cultures, and this talk is very responsive to certain child cues. In early infancy, we observe parents responding even to the baby's unintentional burps and sighs as though they were intentional communication. Parents also pay close attention to what the infant or young child is seeing or hearing and parent responds with words and sentences that describe the child's experience such as

"Oh, you hear that doggie barking, don't you?", or "You're watching daddy now, eh?"

Autonomous Language Style. Another characteristic of these verbal interactions is the way in which they reflect the "low-context" nature of American culture. As described earlier in this text, communication in most ethnic groups is much more context-dependent than among the United States middle class. That is, meaning is derived and communicated through shared experiences, body language, and so on, instead of through direct explicit verbal messages that can stand alone (Hecht, Andersen, and Ribeau, 1989). In high-context cultures, there is less demand for children to understand or use highly specific language unaccompanied by nonverbal or situational cues. Communication takes place around situations and events that are already shared and understood, or the communication is accompanied by facial expressions and gestures which assist in communicating the message. In middle-class homes, there is relatively greater emphasis on helping children learn to communicate clearly with *words alone*. This is sometimes referred to as "autonomous" language or "literate style" language. The specific strategies that parents use to facilitate development of these verbal skills are described in Chapter 5.

Object Reference and Labeling. Another interesting characteristic of mainstream parent-child interactions is somewhat related to the autonomous language use described above. This is the frequency with which parents refer to *objects* in the immediate physical environment. Several studies have demonstrated the relatively greater reference to three-dimensional objects which are seen, heard, touched, and moved (Bornstein, Tal, & Tamis-LeMonda, 1991). Middle-class United States parents frequently say the names of things. They repeatedly refer to toys, utensils, food, articles of clothing, pets, furniture, and so on, present in the immediate environment. For example, a parent at dinner time may say, "Here's your *fork* and your *spoon* and your *bowl*. Eat your *carrots* with your *fork*, not with your *spoon*." It is easy to see how this pattern facilitates the development of highly specific, exact, autonomous style language. Every "thing" has its own exact name.

Eventually, the child learns that saying a particular word refers to that exact object, even if the object is not present. This is what is meant by "low-context" communication. Words can stand alone, even without contextual cues.

As with so many other communicative interactions we have mentioned, this is relatively uncommon among other cultures. This pattern of reference also contributes to mainstream children becoming very object oriented; for example, they are used to playing with toys, blocks, pots, and pans. As an early childhood professional, you must understand how different this may be from children from nonmainstream cultures, and what the ramifications of this difference are. First, early childhood center-based programs are designed around *physical materials* with which children are expected to engage and explore. Children from nonmainstream families may not be motivated by these materials. They may be more interested in social interactions, tactile kinesthetic experiences, music, and observing others play. It is important for early interventionists to realize that virtually all United States assessment instruments rely heavily on test items that evaluate children's interactions with objects. Indeed, the "object concept" is absolutely central to Western theories and conceptualizations of normal development.

This is not to suggest that children from nonmainstream cultures do not develop object concepts. However, their relative preference for play activities and for contexts in which to engage in exploration may not focus primarily on toys and other objects. In fact, even within middle-class American families, there are children whose temperaments and cognitive styles dictate that they are not particularly object oriented. One of the author's daughters never played with toys or other objects until she was old enough to pretend the toys were interacting socially with each other!

Independence and Assertiveness. The value of independence has an important influence on parents' view of language development. Parents value their children's learning to talk, and the earlier the better. They also expect children to be able to tell stories and give verbal explanations well before formal schooling begins. Families also have a tolerance for verbal assertiveness (arguing, saying "no") which is considered aggressive and unacceptable in other cultures.

Another example of mainstream families' push for independence is in the practice of placing very young babies in their own bed, often in a room separate from the parents. In many other cultures this is unheard of, and would be tantamount to child abuse (see McKenna, 2000 for a discussion of cultural issues and influences on infant sleep patterns). Mainstream culture frowns on infants sleeping in the parent's bed although this is a common practices in many non-mainstream cultures. In addition, parental expectations that babies should sleep through the night are considered inappropriate in other cultures (Super & Harkness, 1982). Again, these practices clearly reflect the value of early independence.

There is also a push to achieve other developmental milestones as early as possible, for example self-feeding and walking. Mainstream babies are weaned very early, relative to most other cultures. They are encouraged to begin finger feeding even though they do not have the necessary motor skills and are very messy. While most mothers consider food in children's hair (and eyes and nose) to be repugnant, mainstream mothers are less concerned by it if the child is learning to feed himself. If you are working in an early intervention program with infants, you may find your goal of finger feeding for a developmentally delayed child is not supported by the parents. It is important to work out some compromise concerning this issue; for example, initially working on it only in the center-based program rather than at home, or avoiding messy foods.

Parents frequently spend time encouraging children to walk, long before they are physically ready. Early physical and motor development are valued by other cultures as well, such as by African American families.

This assistance and encouragement to achieve milestones and master tasks in mainstream culture is sometimes referred to as "achievement press." This parental pressure is eventually incorporated into the adult psyche.

Summary. It is important to realize that the mainstream values of children's talkativeness and autonomous language skills, independence, and rapid development, as well as parenting styles that are egalitarian and responsive to children's communicative behaviors, are relatively unique when compared to many other cultures. The sections below summarize the literature that describes child-rearing characteristics of several cultural groups. It is extremely important to realize, however, that any given family with whom you are working may demonstrate *all* or *none* of the characteristics which are said to be typical of their particular cultural group. Saying that a particular child-rearing practices is typical of a certain group simply means that a higher proportion of families in that group demonstrate that practice compared to families from another group.

African American Families

Coping with Racism.   As mentioned earlier in this text, several authors have suggested that in African American culture, probably the single most significant theme in child rearing is teaching young children, especially males, to cope with racism (Peters, 1985). They are taught the importance of achievement, to have self-esteem, and to understand their African American heritage and identity."Black parents are aware of the necessity of imparting a message regarding ethnicity and self-esteem to their children in preparation for the expected encounters with racism" (Harrison, 1985, p. 189).

Independence and Individualism.   Despite a strong loyalty to the extended family and relatively authoritarian parenting styles, African American families, like mainstream families, value the development of independence and assertiveness as well as individualism. Children are not discouraged from developing their own style and personality. Early independence in skills such as walking and dressing are encouraged, and children take on responsibility for household chores and childcare at much earlier ages than children from mainstream families.

Self-respect is a critical value in African American culture. The importance of children being able to defend themselves, as reported in the study by Hale

(Hale-Benson, 1986) described earlier in this chapter, is an example of a strategy used to ensure children's self-respect.

Kinship.   An important value in African American family is the notion of kinship. Ones "kin" or "folks" may include blood relatives and good friends. Reliance on this extended kinship system has important survival value for African American families. Young children learn to identify kinship relationships and to value the persons who are "their people" (Willis, 1998).

Also important in many African American communities is the *in loco parentis* role played by adults. Historically—although less so today (Willis, 1998)—all adults have the collective responsibility for correcting or disciplining children.

The multiple caregivers whom children often experience in their extended kinship systems are often sources of concern to early childhood educators. The practice is viewed as creating problems related to inconsistent caregiving and lack of predictability in the child's environment. However, particularly in economically and socially stressed neighborhoods, the flexibility and availability of many caregivers is absolutely essential to children's survival. The traditional mainstream nuclear family structure, because of its relative isolation, cannot thrive without ample financial and material resources. In the absence of such resources, and in the context of neighborhoods considered unpredictable and unsafe, the extended kinship network is an adaptation that has been of great importance to the survival of African American children and families.

Discipline.   Significant differences in discipline strategies are frequent sources of misunderstanding between African American and mainstream cultures. The use of corporal punishment and authoritarian parenting styles are described in the literature as characteristic of African American discipline (Harry, 1992). In a study conducted by Gillum, Gomez-Marin, and Prineas (1984) that surveyed a large sample of midwestern families, African American families differed from whites in several areas: children were less likely to openly express conflict; there was a stronger moral-religious emphasis; and there was more organization and control than in white families.

Early childhood educators and most members of the mainstream culture assume that such authoritarian parenting practices have negative affects on children. Indeed, studies comparing the effects of various parenting styles in middle-class families generally reported that children raised in authoritarian environments may demonstrate developmental problems, particularly in the area of social competence and initiative (Baumrind, 1971) However, it is interesting to note that in Baumrind's (1972) study of African American parents, authoritarian parenting styles, at least for girls, were associated with social competence and initiative. Delpit (1988) suggests that the effects of parenting style come not from whether the style is authoritative or democratic but instead are related to the extent to which the child experiences a loving relationship with the parent.

Nevertheless, if your background reflects a preference for nonauthoritarian, relatively permissive discipline practices, be aware that this difference is a particularly difficult one with which to deal unemotionally. It should also be noted that despite the use of relatively harsh discipline strategies in other cultures (for example, Asian), unconscious racism may contribute to your greater intolerance of its occurrence in African American families.

High-context Communication Style. While verbal expression is highly valued in African American cul-

ture, there are interesting dissimilarities between mainstream and African American language patterns. African American families value a more indirect communication style, very much dependent on shared context, shared history, and shared emotion. Nonverbal communication plays a major role in communicative interactions and is just as important as the verbal aspects of communication. In other words, a wide range of facial expressions, body movements, and gestures are just as important in conveying messages as the actual words spoken.

Also interesting is the avoidance of overexplaining or talking about the obvious. The now classic study by Heath (1983) describes the early adult-child communicative interactions of black families living in rural Appalachia. In this community, it was considered inappropriate to talk directly about the obvious. Therefore, the practice of describing what a child is seeing and doing, so common in mainstream families and in school settings, may be considered to be strange and unnecessary.

Studies that compared the verbal interaction styles of mothers from different cultural groups frequently report a less verbally responsive style among African American mothers. It is important to note that the subjects in many of these studies were from low socioeconomic classes. Studies of middle-class African American families demonstrate communicative patterns more similar to that of mainstream culture (Heath, 1983). Several studies by Field and her associates (Field & Widmayer, 1981) reported significantly lower rates of vocal interaction with infants, less responsive verbalization, less engagement in social games, and less frequent labeling. This is quite possibly related to another of Heath's findings that African American adults do not fully engage in communicative interaction with children until they can talk. This is unlike mainstream mothers who believe they must *teach* their children to talk.

Avoidance of Spoiling. Another major theme in African American families is the avoidance of overindulging or "spoiling" children. The source of this particular value has many roots. It is related partly to an early biblical teaching which says, "He who spareth the rod hateth his son" (Proverbs 13:24). This translates into the familiar dictum, "Spare the rod; spoil the child." It is related also to the need for children to grow up strong and be able to defend themselves physically and emotionally against a hostile society. Finally, there is the belief that, for their own survival, children must learn to obey and respect authority. Caregiving practices that are viewed as "spoiling" children are also generally viewed as incompatible with teaching children to comply and to follow rules.

Although avoidance of spoiling is definitely an issue, it does not suggest that African American families are not nurturing. Infants in African American communities are almost constantly in the midst of social interactions in which they are held and and attended to (Hale-Benson 1986). This constant attention from a variety of adults and older children contributes to the highly social interactional and cognitive styles characteristic of African American children.

Traditional Asian Families

The number of distinct subgroups included under the term "Asian" is overwhelming (Chinese, Japanese, Korean, "Indochinese" including Laotian, Cambodian, Vietnamese, and Malaysian). East Asian Indians and Filipinos might also be included. In many ways, this lumping together of many separate groups is inappropriate. Even within the major Asian cultural groups, such as the Chinese, there are many different subgroups characterized by significant linguistic, social, and political differences.

Nevertheless, review of the literature describing various "Asian" cultural groups suggests several family and child-rearing characteristics typical across many groups. In part, these reflect the influence of religion and philosophy that have shaped many Asian cultures. Buddhist religious teachings, together with the powerful influence of Confucian philosophy, are particularly important to our understanding of Asian child-rearing practices.

Family as Central Focus. The ultimate value in most Asian cultures is respect for the family. Where the influence of Buddhism is strong, the family not only consists of the current extended family, but also includes all ancestors. A key value that parents must teach their children is the importance of avoiding any action that would shame or disgrace the family. There is a strong focus on "right" behavior and the proper ways to conduct oneself. In addition, children are taught to honor the family, particularly through scholarly achievement. Thus, children are "ingrained with a lifelong respect for knowledge, wisdom, intelligence, and love of learning" (Chan, 1998 p. 293–294). Children learn early that succeeding academically is a major source of honor to the family and a great tribute to their parents. This value has implications for how many Asian families view disability, particularly mental retardation. One common thread that characterizes most Asian cultures are the specifically defined, ascribed roles of individual family members.

Hierarchical Family Structure.   Asian families are "patrilineal;" that is, they are defined and extended through the fathers' family, and the father has ultimate authority. This is not to suggest, however, that mothers do not play important roles. In many Asian cultures, while the husband is clearly the head of the family, his primarily responsibility lies outside the home. Mothers take responsibility for all matters inside the home, including child rearing and finances. In the Vietnamese culture, children view the mother as having equal status with that of the father (Te, 1989).

One of the greatest differences from mainstream family structure is the rigid ascription of roles and rank. One's status in the family is determined by age and gender. Beginning with the father, oldest males have greatest rights and responsibilities. Learning to conform to one's role in the family hierarchy is an important goal of childhood. In addition, the teachings of Buddha value strict self-control over behavior and emotional expression.

The conformity and control that result from these values and practices is a major source of culture clash with mainstream United States society. Mainstream families emphasize individualism, egalitarian relationships, role flexibility, and honest expression of feelings and opinions. These mainstream values are clearly evident in preschool and child-care settings. For example, children are encouraged to express their feelings, even when they are negative feelings such as fear and anger. They are encouraged to negotiate conflicts with peers rather than obey the strict authority of adults. Adults often play and interact with children as though they were peers. Asian families—adults as well as children— may experience discomfort in such environments. In their own social environments, there is little ambiguity about ways of behaving. There are clear rules for nearly all social situations. Should an unusual or ambiguous situation arise, there is always someone of higher status who provides direction.

"Filial Piety" and Reciprocity. The tradition of "filial piety" is central to the focus on family respect in Asian families (Te, 1989). Chan (1998) describes filial piety as "unquestioning loyalty and obedience to parents and concern for and understanding of their needs and wishes" (p. 258). Filial piety also extends to the need to respect ancestors as well as authority figures. As a result, families are not likely to disagree with or assert their own opinions in their interactions with early childhood professionals. They also may have difficulty respecting early childhood workers who do not present themselves in a professional, authoritative manner.

Other Confucian values, critical to the understanding of filial piety, are the concepts of "reciprocity" and obligation. For example, parents sacrifice to meet children's needs. In turn, children are obligated to obey parents and honor them through proper behavior and achievement. Another example is demonstrated in what Chan (1998) refers to as a classic response to a sibling disagreement. The parent scolds the older sibling for failing to set a good example and the younger child for lack of respect for the older sibling.

Communication Patterns. Because of the importance of obedience and respect for rank, and because of the absolute authority of the father, there is very little interactive communication between adults and children in Asian families (other than the interactions of early infancy that will be discussed later). Generally, adults speak and children listen. Children's silence is a sign of respect and attention. When communication occurs it is often indirect and nonverbal, and confrontation is always avoided. Thus, young children are not encouraged to initiate communication. Also because of the value of modesty and humility, young children are not praised for their accomplishments. The absence of criticism indicates approval. Some Asian families are uncomfortable with the frequent praise given children in early childhood programs. Young Asian children may not respond to praise in the same way that mainstream children do. Until they become accustomed to it, praise and attention for performance may make them uncomfortable or embarrassed.

Mother-Infant Interactions.   In mainstream culture, the newborn is viewed as very dependent and the goal is to encourage independence. Just the opposite is true in many Asian families. Infants must learn to be dependent. The baby's needs are anticipated to discourage crying or initiating requests. Some Asian cultures believe that babies must be protected from evil spirits. For example, according to Chan (1998), the Hmong avoid naming a baby for two years so the spirits cannot find it. If a baby becomes ill, Cambodian parents temporarily change the baby's name to confuse the spirits.

Because babies are considered a "gift from the gods," they are protected and nurtured by adults. Their environment is typically nurturant, secure, and predictable. During the period of infancy, parents are permissive. Babies often sleep with the mother and adults react immediately to infant needs.

Mothers interact with babies but in ways different from mainstream mothers. Interaction may be more physical than verbal, and is not usually object-oriented. In a study reported by Bornstein, Tal, & Tamis-LeMonda (1991), Japanese mothers were socially interactive with their infants in ways similar to American mothers, but were much less likely to include object references in their interactions. The mainstream United States pattern of attention to objects in the environment and labeling of "things" emerge as fairly unique.

The Preschool Period: Discipline and Responsibility.   As children move from infancy to preschool age there is a major shift from indulgence and affection to discipline and education (Chan, 1998; Chhim, 1989). Children have increasing responsibility to behave properly. You, in your role as an early childhood professional, must attempt to understand what is considered "proper behavior" in a particular family. Determine if you have certain expectations for a child's behavior that are inconsistent with parental expectations.

In some Asian cultures (for example, Cambodia) (Chhim, 1989), preschool girls assume certain child-care and housework responsibilities. Children learn these skills mostly through imitation. Some groups, for example, Laotian families, avoid giving direct guidance despite the value placed on learning proper behavior. Learning takes place primarily through observation of others (Luangpraseut, 1989).

Child-Rearing in Families from Latino Backgrounds

Families with Latino backgrounds originate from different Spanish-speaking countries and reflect a wide range along the continuum of acculturation (Ramirez, 1989; Zuniga, 1998). Despite this heterogeneity, however, certain family values remain well-entrenched, particularly in Mexican-American families.

Primacy of the Family. As is the case with most non-mainstream cultures, families with Latino roots are predominantly collectivist. The primary focus of most Latino groups is on the family and extended kinship ties (Ramirez, 1989; Zuniga, 1998). There is strong reliance on the family for support. Family consists not only of extended relatives, but also includes *compadres*, or godparents, who play important roles in the family. To facilitate the cohesion of the extended family, value is placed on affiliation and cooperation. Confrontation and competition are discouraged. According to Zuniga (1998), fighting among siblings is not acceptable; expression of negative emotions by women also is discouraged.

Child rearing emphasizes conforming to conventions, respect for authority figures (including older family members) and the importance of family identity. Compared to mainstream families, much less emphasis is placed on achievement of developmental milestones and competitiveness. It is important for early childhood educators to realize that normative data for achievement of developmental milestones are derived primarily from mainstream, Anglo populations of children whose parents are achievement-oriented. Middle-class mainstream parents are very aware of approximate ages at which children reach developmental milestones and push their children to reach these milestones *earlier* than the norm. Latino families may be less aware of these developmental norms, and, even if they are aware of them, do not push children to gain a competitive edge over other children.

"Personalismo."   One of the strongest values that characterize families with Latino roots is the concept of *personalismo,* or "personalism;" that is, the importance of interpersonal relationships. Warm, individualized, responsive, and respectful interactions with others reflect this value. Zuniga (1998) points out that service providers must develop an interpersonally oriented style different from the task-oriented style that typically characterizes mainstream professional interactions. In your own work, you may believe that "professional" interactions should not include personal chit chat with parents. However, Latino families (and Asian families as well) may find beginning a conversation with business matters, (for example, a child's attendance record, the details of your early education program, requirements for parent participation) are very impersonal. Latino families respect the practice of platicando, a style of informal, friendly chatting that establishes a certain social ambience in which the more serious work takes place (Zuniga, 1998). This is similar to southern United States conversational style that requires the exchange of pleasantries and small talk before attending to the business at hand.

"According to the traditional Hispanic values of personalismo, it is not ability but, rather, goodness and the quality of personal relationships that are important in life" (Levine & Padilla, 1980, p. 34) For many Latino families, being socially well-educated is more important than being academically well-educated. Children learn to be sensitive to others' feelings, to be polite and responsive to elders, to engage in social conversation, and to be personally loyal to friends and family. A child who is *bien educada* is one who learns to understand the importance of relating to others with respect and dignity (Zuniga, 1998)

Family Structure and Roles. As with other non-mainstream groups, Latino homes may include extended family members. Elder members have status and are treated with respect. The mother's role is the self-sacrificing nurturer. In Latino families, the role of mother and *el amor de madre* (motherly love) is much more important than the role of wife. The existence of children validates the marriage (Ramirez, 1989). The marital relationship is built around caring and providing for children. Therefore, particularly during early child-rearing years, couples do not engage in many activities apart from their children.

An important value within traditional Latino families is the role of the father. Latino families are patriarchal. The father has the ultimate responsibility for the well-being of the family; his personal honor is at stake. These are the concepts of *machismo*. The term also connotes a negative image of exaggerated masculinity, sexual virility, and aggressiveness (Trankina, 1983). While "maleness" is certainly part of the concept of machismo, the traditional focus of this value is on the authority and responsibility of adult males as protectors and providers, particularly vis-à-vis family welfare.

The oldest son in Latino families often is encouraged to be dominant and independent. Girls, on the other hand, are restricted in order to protect their innocence until marriage. In general, Latino families are more restrictive than mainstream families (McClintock, Bayard, & McClintock, 1983). For example, children are encouraged to play at home with siblings instead of going to the homes of peers, and usually, they may not stay out late at night.

The influence of machismo has been diminished by the processes of acculturation. Many Latino families now share in household and economic responsibilities, and decision-making. Nevertheless, it is extremely important that you are sensitive to the roles of important male figures in Latino families. Zuniga (1998) suggests that when both husband and wife are present, you should speak to the husband first. Even if a child's father is not present, make sure he is in agreement with recommendations and program plans.

Parent-Child Interaction.   During infancy and the early childhood years, the home is very child-centered. Both parents are usually fairly permissive and indulgent, though even during the early years there is an emphasis on good behavior. During this period, the father is playful and affectionate with young children. As in most cultures, as children get older, they are expected to behave properly and assume more and more responsibility. The Latino father's role then shifts to authority figure and disciplinarian (Ramirez, 1989).

Parent-child interaction is characterized by close physical contact and frequent touching. It is not unusual for older children to sit on mother's lap. Physical contact among family members is important, regardless of age and sex.

Latino parents are more likely to use modeling and demonstration as a teaching strategy instead of specific verbal explanations that are typical of mainstream families. As are most nonmainstream cultures, Latinos are high-context, rather than low-context, communicators. Both verbal and nonverbal communication takes place within the immediate context of experience.

Mothers usually do not view infant communication as intentional during the first year of life (Westby, 1985). Consequently, there is somewhat less contingent responsivity to infant vocal behavior than in mainstream mothers' interactions. Although they may be somewhat less vocally responsive, this is not to suggest that mothers do not talk to their babies. They make frequent use of "attentionals" such as saying the baby's name or making certain nonspeech sounds (Vigil, 1993) to get the baby's attention. Vigil also found that mothers interacted quite differently with baby boys and girls.

In an interesting contrast to mainstream mothers who speak more slowly to infants, Latino women tend to speak more rapidly and to repeat phrases exactly over and over (for example, *"Dame tu mano Dame tu mano Dame tu mano!"*—*"Give me your hand"*). As babies get older, mothers use modeling to instruct them how to make a particular social response to another person, such as *"Dile 'Gracias'"* (*"Say 'Thank you'"*) (Eisenberg, 1982).

Relative to mainstream families, there is a greater emphasis on encouraging young children to engage in social communication instead of learning to label objects and use specific referential language to explain and describe. This emphasis is consistent with the strong cultural value placed on interpersonal relationships that characterizes Latino families.

Child Rearing in Native American Cultures

The cultural group referred to as Native American actually consists of many separate tribes. These tribes speak over 200 different tribal languages (Leap, 1981). There are over 500 federally recognized Native American groups in the United States (LaFromboise & Low, 1989). While these groups each have their own customs, history, and spiritual beliefs, certain commonalities exist related to child-rearing values and practices.

Community Support. Native Americans, like most societies with non-European roots, are collectivist rather than individualistic. However, the primary emphasis is not exclusively on the extended family, but rather on the community and the tribe. The elders in the tribe are important figures in the family's life and friends play important roles in the family's support system. When visiting a Native American home, it is not unusual to find several adults present, both family and nonfamily members. It is important to understand that *all* these adults play important roles in the rearing of young children (Anderson & Fenichel, 1989) For example, a nonfamily friend may be an important source of information about child caregiving and health. The family may identify a spokesperson to represent the family to outsiders. Aunts and uncles may play the roles of teachers and/or disciplinarians. Often, parents are not the primary disciplinarians. After early infancy, grandmothers and aunts may assume key child care roles with young children. All family members, including siblings, assist with child rearing. In some tribes, men share in child care responsibilities (LaFromboise & Low, 1989). Grandparents and tribal elders receive the greatest respect and authority in the community (Anderson & Fenichel, 1989).

According to LaFromboise & Low (1989), the lines of communication in families may be indirect. For example, if a child misbehaves, the parent discusses the behavior with an aunt or uncle who counsels or disciplines the child. Indirect communication also is used for expressing praise. The positive achievement or event is announced by someone in the community instead of by parents so the family's humility can be maintained.

Spirituality and Ceremony.   Spirituality and ceremony are central in the values and daily lives of traditional Native American families, and even in the lives of families who have experienced significant acculturation. Children are viewed as gifts from the gods. A child born with a disability may be the result of the mother who broke a certain taboo during the pregnancy. Some tribes believe that giving too many compliments to a baby or young child brings harm from the gods. In addition, certain replicas such as dolls, pictures, and insignias are considered bad luck (Joe & Malach, 1998). Ceremonies are used to mark important developmental milestones such as the child's first smile or first steps. Tribal ceremonies play critical roles in Native American family life, and often take precedence over nontribal activities such as school attendance. Healing ceremonies are critical to child rearing, even more so if a child has a disability or chronic health problem. These ceremonies may place certain markings or objects on the child's body (Joe & Malach, 1998).

Early childhood professionals must accept the importance of ceremony and ritual in the everyday lives of many Native American children, and find ways to integrate these into early education and intervention programs. For example, before beginning a new program or therapeutic treatment, a family might wish to have a special ceremony. The family or community would ask the spirits to ensure the success of the treatment. In this way, the two cultures work together to maximize the positive effects on the child and family.

Views of Child Development.   Because children are given to families by the gods, family members cherish the time spent caring for and playing with young children. Children's personalities and abilities are considered fixed at birth and permanent. Native American culture has a great respect for "what is" (Anderson &

Fenichel, 1989). Traditionally, Native American communities have integrated children with disabilities into the community although, according to Anderson and Fenichel (1989), greater exposure to mainstream society has resulted in greater stigmatization of persons with disabilities within these communities. Families are reluctant to change children's characteristics. As a result, families are ambivalent about early intervention programs for children with disabilities, and according to Joe and Malach (1998) are reluctant to discipline disabled children. Children's mistakes are tolerated, and in traditional families, there is little use of punishment, particularly physical punishment.

Developmental milestones are regarded as important events for celebration with special ceremonies. However, there is relatively little concern regarding the ages at which these milestones take place. There is little pressure for children to achieve or perform (LaFromboise & Low, 1989). Competitiveness is contrary to the Native American values of group identity and cooperation.

In many tribes, autonomy, in the sense of children being able to manage themselves, has great value. Young children make many decisions and operate independently from an early age (LaFromboise & Low, 1989). Early childhood professionals may view Native American parents as overly permissive and neglectful.

Parent-Child Interaction. Probably the most striking difference between mainstream and Native American families with regard to parent-child interaction is the relative lack of verbal communication. Mothers are usually very quiet with their babies. Their babies are also quiet and easy going. Mothers do not respond to infant vocalizations as though they were communicative, although they are quick to adjust to infant signs of distress by touching the baby and shifting his or her position. An interesting study by Fajardo & Freeman (1981) found that Navajo babies were actually more likely to turn away from their mothers when they stimulated them vocally, whereas Anglo babies were more likely to make eye contact and vocalize. Even in interactions with adults, according to Joe and Malach (1998), Native Americans place more emphasis on how people behave than on what they say.

Typically, young children are not expected to speak to adults. Most communicative interaction takes place with siblings and peers. According to Werner (1984), this pattern encourages group affiliation and interdependence among peers, instead of individuality and attention to and from adults. As an early childhood professional, you need to include older siblings in discussions and demonstrations of communicative interactions with young children because they are more likely to engage in this kind of interaction than are adults.

Learning does not take place primarily through adult responsivity to child cues or through direct verbal explanation and teaching. Communication in Native American tribal cultures is primarily high-context, relying heavily on children learning through observation of adults and older siblings. A primary goal of child rearing is preparation for adult roles.

Stories and Legends.   As children get older, adults' use of stories and legends become an important vehicle for teaching values and proper behavior, as well as handing down the history and values of the tribe. Elements of stories are referred to repeatedly to remind children of certain points or to modify their behaviors (Tafoya, 1983). Stories help demonstrate the important value of harmony and relationships among all elements of life and the spiritual world. Tafoya points out that Native American stories often facilitate perceiving things in different ways, and understanding that life is not fixed or static and thus must be understood through different vantage points. This way of viewing the world differs significantly from mainstream classrooms in which there are specific descriptions and definitions of reality.

The following are examples of tribal teachings excerpted from a book by Stan Padilla (1992). These, in the tribal elders' own words, reflect many of the child-rearing views we have discussed.

> Training began with children who were taught to sit still and enjoy it. They were taught to use their organs of smell, to look when there was apparently nothing to see, and to listen internally when all seemingly was quiet. A child that cannot sit still is a half-developed child. (p. 15)

—Luther Standing Bear
Lakota Sioux

The true Hopi People preserve the sacred knowledge about the way of the earth because the true
Hopi People know that the earth is a living . . .
growing person . . .and all things on it are her
children. (p. 17)

—From the Hopi Declaration of Peace

My father went on talking to me in a low voice.
This is how our people always talk to children,
So low and quiet, the child thinks he is dreaming.
But he never forgets. (p. 18)

—Maria Chona
Papago

❖ SUMMARY

The purpose of this chapter has *not* been to stereotype
the child-rearing practices of different ethnic and racial
groups. Rather the purpose of chapter was to bring
home the point that your views of what constitutes
"normal" and "good" child rearing may be quite different from the views and practices of families who do
not share your culture. If you are a member of the
United States mainstream middle-class culture, you are
likely to place a strong value on child rearing that encourages children's achievement of developmental
milestones, particularly in the areas of physical and
language development. You want your children to be
smart and assertive—capable of using language to
explain and persuade—and you nurture their individualism and self-expression. You expect them to be competitive but nonsexist. Your approach to parenting and
discipline is democratic and egalitarian. You value
"time." You organize your children's daily lives around
clock time. Events of the daily routine occur at approximately the same time. Children have bedtimes, napti-
mes, bathtime, and storytimes.

You buy your children toys. You expect them to
play with "things." You provide specific labels for
these "things" and encourage children to learn to narrate the daily events and describe the world around
them. You believe we help children learn through responsive communication and explanation. You encourage your children to converse with you as though
you were equals.

You believe that you can, through knowledge and determination, change what is. You can intervene and ameliorate children's disabilities and delays and emotional problems.

It is difficult to accept that these practices and values may not be considered particularly important by nonwestern, nonmainstream cultures. Moreover, many of these are considered inappropriate and may be viewed negatively. In most other cultures, what is most important is the support, honor, and extension of the family, not the achievements and expression of an individual child. Families may be ambivalent about the appropriateness of early intervention and early schooling. Even for those families who believe adults play an important teaching role, what is taught is proper social behavior and respect, not better language skills or how to ride a bike.

Individuals from many nonmainstream cultures are not dominated by time. They live in the present, not the future. They do not obsess about the child's schedule for the week or help him or her do better in the future.

Quietness, emotional control, and saving face are important values conveyed to children in many families instead of verbosity, sharing ones feelings, and "telling it like it is."

And yet, within all parents is a driving force to achieve and maintain the well-being of their children. That is where you, as an early childhood professional,

can find your common ground with all families. The process of sharing and understanding one another's views on how best to achieve this well-being requires mutual respect, communication, flexibility, and patience.

❖ REFERENCES

Anastasiow, N. (1986). Cultural differences in the development of meanings and use of language. In N. Anastasiow (ed.), *Development and Disability* (pp. 183–209). Baltimore: Paul H. Brookes Publishing.

Anderson, P., & Fenichel, E. (1989). *Serving culturally diverse families of infants and toddlers with disabilities.* Washington DC: National Center for Clinical Infant Programs.

Baumrind, D. (1971). Current patterns of parental authority. *Developmental Psychology Monographs, 4,* (1, part 2).

Baumrind, D. (1972). An exploratory study of socialization effects on Black children: Some Black-White comparisons. *Child Development, 43,* 261–267.

Bornstein, M. H., Tal, J., & Tamis-LeMonda, C. S. (1991). Parenting in cross-cultural perspective: The United States, France and Japan. In M. H. Bornstein (ed.), *Cultural approaches to parenting* (pp. 69–90). Hillsdale, NJ: Lawrence Erlbaum Associates, Publishers.

Boykin, W., & Toms, F. (1985). Black child socialization. In H. P. McAdoo & J. L. McAdoo (eds.), *Black children: Social, educational and parental environments.* Beverly Hills: Sage Publications.

Briggs, C. L. (1984). Learning how to ask: Native metacommunicative competence and the incompetence of fieldworkers. *Language in Society, 13,* 1–28.

Bruner, J. (1982). The organization of action and the nature of the adult-infant transaction. In E. Tronick (ed.), *Social interchange in infancy: Affect, cognition and communication* (pp. 23–35). Baltimore: University Park Press.

Chan, S. (1998). Families with Asian roots. In M. Hanson & E. Lynch (eds.), *Developing cross-cultural competence: A guide for working with young children and their families* (2nd ed). Baltimore: Paul Brookes Publishing.

Chinn, P. C., & Wong, G. Y. (1992). Recruiting and retaining Asian/Pacific American Teachers. In M. E. Dilworth (ed.), *Diversity in Teacher Education.* San Francisco: Jossey-Bass.

Chhim, Sun-Him. (1989). *Introduction to Cambodian culture.* San Diego: San Diego State University Multifunctional Service Center.

Deloache, J., & Gottlieb, A. (2000). *A world of babies. Imagined childcare guides for seven societies.* New York: Cambridge University Press.

Delpit, L. (1988). The silenced dialogue: Power and pedagogy in educating other people's children. *Harvard Educational Review, 58*(3), 280–298.

Eisenberg, A. (1982). Language development in cultural perspective: Talk in three Mexicano homes. Unpublished Ph.D. dissertation. University of California, Berkeley.

Fajardo, B. F., & Freedman, D. G. (1981). Maternal rhythmicity in three American cultures. In T. M. Field, A. M. Soctek, P. Vietze, & P. H. Leiderman (eds.), *Culture and early interactions.* Hillsdale, NJ: Lawrence Erlbaum Associates.

Feuerstein, R., Rand, Y., Hoffman, M., & Miller, R. (1980). *Instrumental enrichment.* Baltimore: University Park Press.

Field, T., & Widmayer, S. M. (1981). Mother-infant interactions among lower SES Black, Cuban, Puerto Rican & South American immigrants. In T. M. Field, A. M. Sostek, P. Vietze, & P. H. Leiderman (eds.), *Culture and early interactions.* Hillsdale, NJ: Lawrence Erlbaum Associates.

Franklin, A., & Boyd-Franklin, N. (1985). A psychoeducational perspective on Black parenting. In H. P. McAdoo & J. L. McAdoo (eds.), *Black children: Social, eductional and parental environments.* Beverly Hills: Sage Publications.

Gallimore, R., Weisner, T. S., Kaufman, S., & Bernheimer, L. P. (1989). The social construction of ecocultural niches: Family accommodation of developmentally delayed children. *American Journal on Mental Retardation,* 94, 216–230.

Gallup Report. (1989, September). *Religion in America.*

Gillum, R., Gomez-Marin, O., & Prineas, R. (1984). Racial differences in personality, behavior, and family environment in Minneapolis school children. *Journal of the National Medical Association,* 76, 1097–1105.

Hale-Benson, J. (1986). *Black children: Their roots, culture and learning style.* Baltimore: The Johns Hopkins University Press.

Hale, J. (1991). The transmission of cultural values to young African American children. *Young Children, 46*(6), 7–15.

Hanson, M. (1998). Families with Anglo-European roots. In M. Hanson & E. Lynch (eds.), *Developing cross-cultural competence: A guide to working with young children and their families* (2nd ed) (pp. 93–126). Baltimore: Paul H. Brookes Publishing.

Harrison, A. O. (1985). The Black family's socializing environment. In H. P. McAdoo & J. L. McAdoo (eds.), *Black children: Social, educational and parental environments.* Beverly Hills: Sage Publications.

Harry, B. (1992). Developing cultural self-awareness: The first step in values clarification for early interventionists. *Topics in Early Childhood Special Education, 12*(3), 333–350.

Heath, S. B. (1983). *Ways with words: Language, life and work in communities and classrooms.* Cambridge, England: Cambridge University Press.

Hecht, M. L., Andersen, P. A., & Ribeau, S. A. (1989). The cultural dimensions of non-verbal communication. In M. K. Asante & W. B. Gudykunst (eds.), *Handbook of international and intercultural communication* (pp. 163–185). Newbury Park, CA: Sage Publications.

Joe, J. R., & Malach, R. S. (1998). Families with native American roots. In M. Hanson & E. Lynch (eds.) *Devel-*

oping cross-cultural competence (2nd ed) (pp. 127–164). Baltimore: Paul H. Brookes Publishing.

Kohn, M. L. (1977). *Class and conformity* (2nd ed.). Chicago: University of Chicago Press.

LaFromboise, T. D., & Low, K. G. (1989). American Indian children and adolescents. In J. Gibbs & L. Huang (eds.) *Children of color* (pp. 114–147). San Francisco: Jossey-Bass Publishers.

Leap, W. L. (1981). American Indian language maintenance. *Annual Review of Anthropology*, 10, 271–280.

Levine, R. A. (1974). Parental goals: A cross cultural view. In H. J. Leichter (ed.), *The family as educator.* New York: Teachers College Press.

Levine, E. S., & Padilla, A. M. (1980). *Crossing cultures in therapy: Pluralistic counseling for the Hispanic.* Pacific Grove, CA: Brooks Cole.

Luangpraseut, Khamchong, (1989). *Laos, culturally speaking.* San Diego: San Diego State University Multifunctional Service Center.

McClintock, E., Bayard, M. P., & McClintock, C. G. (1983). The socialization of social motivation in Mexican American families. In E. E. Garcia (ed.), *The Mexican American child: Language, cognition, and social development* (pp. 143–162). Tempe, AZ: Arizona State University: Center for Bilingual Education.

McKenna, J. J. (2000). Cultural influences on infant and childhood sleep biology, and the science that studies it. *Zero to Three, 20*(3), 9–18.

Mann, T. (2000). The impact of values on parenting: Reflections in a "scientific" age. *Zero to Three, 20*(3), 3–8.

Norton, D. G. (1990). Understanding the early experience of Black children in high risk environments: Culturally and ecologically relevant research as a guide to support for families. *Zero-to-Three, Vol X*(4), 1–7.

Ochs, E. (1982). Talking to children in Western Samoa. *Language in Society*, 11, 77–104.

Ogbu, J. V. (1974). *The next generation.* New York: Academic Press.

Padilla, S. (1992). *A natural education. Native American ideas and thoughts.* Summertown, TN: Book Publishing Co.

Peters, M. (1985). Racial socializatiion of young black children. In H. P. McAdoo & J. L. McAdoo (eds.), *Black children: Social, educational and parental environments.* Beverly Hills: Sage Publications.

Phillips, C. B. (1994). The movement of African-American children through sociocultural contests: A case of conflict resolution. In B. L. Mallory and R. S. New (eds). *Diversity and developmentally appropriate practices* (pp. 137–154). New York: Teachers College Press.

Quinn, R. (1995). Early intervention? Que quiere eso? What does that mean? In H. Kayser (ed.), Bilingual speech-language pathology. An Hispanic focus (pp. 75–91). San Diego: Singular Press.

Ramirez, O. (1989). Mexican American Children and adolescents. In J. Gibbs & L. Huang (eds.), *Children of color* (pp. 224–250). San Francisco: Jossey-Bass Publishers.

Super, C. M., & Harkness, S. (1982) The infant's niche in rural Kenya and metropolitan America. In L. Adler (ed.), *Issues in cross-cultural research*. New York: Academic Press.

Tafoya, T. (1983). Coyote in the classroom. The use of Native American oral tradition with young children. In O. N. Saracho & B. Spodek (eds.), Understanding the multi-cultural experience in early childhood education (pp. 35–44). Washington, DC: National Association for the Education of Young Children.

Taylor, R. (1994). Black American families. In R. Taylor (ed.), Minority families in the United States: A multicultural perspective (pp. 19–46). Englewood Cliffs, NJ: Prentice Hall.

Te, Huynh Dinh. (1989). *Introduction to Vietnamese culture*. San Diego: San Diego State University Multifunctional Service Center.

Trankina, F. (1983). Clinical issues and techniques in working with Hispanic children and their families. In G. J. Powell, J. Yamamoto, A. Romero, & A. Morales (eds.), *The psychosocial development of minority group children*. New York: Brunner Mazel.

Van Leeuwen, M. S. (1990). *Gender and Grace*. Downers Grove, IL: Intervarsity Press.

Vigil, D. (1993). Gender differences in Mexican-American mothers' vocalizations to their young infants. Unpublished Masters Thesis. Los Angeles: California State University, Los Angeles.

Vygotsky, L. (1978). *Mind in society: The development of higher psychological processes*. Cambridge, MA: Harvard University Press.

Weisner, T. S., Beizer, L., & Stolze, L. (1991). Religion and families of children with developmental delays. *American Journal on Mental Deficiency, 95*(6), 647–662.

Werner, E. (1984). *Child care: Kith, kin and hired hands*. Baltimore: University Park Press.

Westby, C. (1985, November). Cultural differences in Caregiver-child interaction: Implications for assessment and intervention. Paper presented at National Convention of the American Speech-Language-Hearing Association. Albuquerque, New Mexico.

Willis, W. (1998). Families with African-American roots. In M. Hanson & E. Lynch (eds.), *Developing cross-cultural competence: A guide for working with young children and their families* (2nd ed) (pp. 165–207). Baltimore: Paul H. Brookes Publishing.

Zuniga, M. E. (1998). Families with Latino roots. In M. Hanson & E. Lynch (eds.) *Developing cross-cultural competence* (2nd ed) (pp. 209–250). Baltimore: Paul H. Brookes Publishing.

Zussman, J. N. (1978). Relationship of demographic factors in parental discipline techniques. *Developmental Psychology, 14*, 683–686.

CHAPTER 4

Cultural Influences on Young Children's Social Skills and Behaviors

Family attitudes and values, as well as the child-rearing practices discussed in the previous chapter, have a clear influence on the development of children's social skills and behaviors. As young children from nonmainstream families and communities enter early childhood programs, they bring with them social behaviors and interaction patterns different from those of middle-class children. This chapter examines a number of ways in which cultural values and practices influence young children's social development. These include adult-child interactions, peer interactions, play behaviors, and gender roles. Communication styles, another important area of social development, discussed at length in the next chapter.

Also important in any discussion of children's social development is the development of ethnic and racial identity, stereotypes, and prejudice. A section of this chapter considers the stages of children's development of attitudes toward race and ethnicity (their own and others) as well as strategies for including antibias strategies in early childhood curricula.

Early childhood educators are well-trained in the developmental stages of children's social development and they become sensitized to identifying potential problems in development. Even by age three, young children should be able to separate easily from their primary caregiver, explore and play independently with a variety of toys, be comfortable with other children engaging in "parallel play" alongside them, follow simple instructions initiate interactions with adults to express needs, and engage in rudimentary conversational turn-taking.

Concerns about Linda and Andrew

Mary Fowler is a new early childhood teacher. Her first assignment is in a Head Start classroom with 20 children. Most of the children are Anglo and Mexican-American. There is one Chinese American female and two African-American boys. She spends the first week trying to get to know the children by interacting with them on a one-to-one basis. She is concerned about two of the children: Linda, who is Chinese-American; and Andrew. who is African-American.

Linda seems frightened whenever Ms. Fowler talks to her. She doesn't look at her, never initiates interaction, and almost never expresses her needs. Ms. Fowler decides she needs to look into this child's background for possible indications of emotional problems or abuse.

Andrew is extremely active. He moves quickly around the room from one toy area to another, but does not really play with things. He seems more interested in taunting the other children. He is also aggressive in soliciting Ms. Fowler's attention. When she encourages him to play with the blocks, she is unsuccessful. When she explains things to Andrew, he gives her relatively little feedback to indicate he is listening or understands. She is concerned that Andrew may have some kind of learning disability such as an attention deficit disorder.

It is important to realize that social development is highly susceptible to the socializing influences of families, and eventually, peer groups. Anthropological studies of play, for example, reveal that children's play is different in different cultures (Sutton-Smith & Roberts, 1981). Our western notions of the stages of play development, with its focus on the development of symbolic and creative play, are highly ethnocentric. Child social behaviors that are considered "skills" in one family might be considered totally inappropriate in another. A major challenge for the early childhood professional who works with children from many different cultural backgrounds is to learn to view children's interactions and reactions in the classroom within a cultural context. In the scenario described above, it is important for Ms. Fowler not to jump to conclusions about Linda and Andrew. The next few pages in this chapter provide insights into alternative interpretations of these children's behavior.

❖ ADULT-CHILD INTERACTIONS

One critical area in which children from different backgrounds may vary significantly is how they interact with adults. A child characteristic that is often valued and encouraged in middle-class homes is the ability to interact with adults, even to initiate interactions. For example, the common "Tell Aunt Millie what we did today" scenario begins to set the stage at a very young age for children to feel comfortable interacting with adults. Such interactions are by no means limited to familiar adults. A middle-class mother very well might encourage her young child to tell such a narrative even to someone the child does not know.

Many African American children are also fairly comfortable interacting with adults. Verbal teasing, playful arguing, and "volleying" between mothers and their children are common (Hale-Benson, 1986). However, relative to the white middle-class norm, this behavior may seem aggressive or combative. In some cases, this perception is reinforced by teachers' inability to effectively control African American children. Hale-Benson (1986) suggests that teachers have difficulty controlling African American children because they do not use the highly directive authoritarian parenting style characteristic of many African American families. As a result, children misread or ignore teacher cues.

Another important aspect of adult-child interaction with African American children is the importance of affect (emotionality) in the relationship. African American children are extremely sensitive to emotional elements in an interaction; that is, they are attuned to the adult's feelings toward them. If there is a positive emotional attachment, children will seek out adult one-on-one interaction. Related to this character-

istic are the research findings done in the 1970s on racial bias in standardized testing. These studies demonstrated that black children's test performance was greatly affected by their relationship with the examiner. The relationship had relatively little effect on the performance of white children (Zigler, Abelson, & Seitz, 1973).

Teachers should be aware of the importance of this emotional relationship with African American children. Hale-Benson suggests that teachers facilitate this through expressions of warmth and positive emotions, playful verbal interaction, use of rhythmic speech, and distinctive intonation styles.

Another area in which mainstream children often differ from nonmainstream children is in their use of conversational responses to adults. Middle-class children are taught to hold up their end of the conversation by responding verbally to adults, and by "backchanneling." Backchanneling is providing feedback to the speaker to indicate that the listener is being attentive and following what the speaker is saying. Examples include such comments as "uh huh," "okay," or nonverbal feedback such as nodding the head to indicate attention. Young children from nonmainstream cultures are somewhat less likely to do this (Allen & Majidi-Ahi, 1989).

While mainstream children and African American children are often comfortable interacting with adults, young children from Asian American families, particularly those whose families are influenced by traditional values, may find such interactions difficult. They are more accustomed to formal interactions with adults in which there are clear rules regarding responses expected from children. For example, Asian American children may not be comfortable calling an adult by a first name (Huang & Ying, 1989). Nagata (1989), in describing Japanese American children's social behaviors, suggests that children may even have difficulty playing spontaneously in the presence of adults. Such play behavior may be seen as frivolous by Japanese parents. In addition, it may be too open-ended. The child may be used to waiting for specific requests or cues from adults. The concept of "enryo" is important in many Japanese American families (deferring to authority and not expressing wishes and preferences) (Nagata, 1989, p.79). This emphasis makes it difficult for young Japanese children to feel comfortable in situations such as "free play" where it is unclear what is expected of them.

Cheng (1987) also discusses the Asian child's difficulty interacting with adults. Children may wish to use an intermediary, such as a peer, to communicate with the teacher. Cheng suggests the teacher allow this, but explain that it is okay for the child to approach the teacher directly. Cheng suggests several strategies to help facilitate interaction with Asian children. It is helpful to give explicit rules for what is "good" behavior. The less ambiguity about what is expected, the more comfortable the child will be. Also Cheng suggests that children should be reprimanded privately rather than in front of other children, and teachers should avoid speaking too directly. Children from traditional Asian backgrounds may need assistance in learning to express preferences and make decisions. The teacher begins by frequently presenting the child with very simple choices. For example, "Do you want the blue paint or the red paint?"

Other characteristics that influence adult-child interaction are mentioned by Kitano (1983). For example, Hawaiian children have strong affiliative needs and are more comfortable interacting with groups of children than one-on-one with a teacher. Chinese-American children are often described as highly reflective and as a result, may take a long time to respond to instructions and questions. This delayed responding may be misunderstood by teachers as indicating a lack of understanding. Similarly, some Native American tribes may emphasize the importance of perfection in performing certain tasks. As a result, children may need extended periods of observation before they attempt to perform a new activity (LaFromboise & Low, 1989)

Mexican-American children are taught to respect adults and comply with their requests. McClintock, et al. (1983) discuss the role of family size on children's socialization. The larger family size of many Mexican American families requires children be assigned specific roles and responsibilities within the family where there are strict rules related to conflict regulation. (Such rules are also important for maintaining harmony in many Asian-American families.) As a result, Mexican-American children are much less likely than Anglo children to talk back or contradict adults. There is great emphasis in Mexican American homes to teach children to be well-behaved, responsible, and considerate of others. Altruism is an important theme in many Mexican-American homes (McClintock et al., 1983). Children are taught to behave properly and to consider the effects of their behavior on others (Saracho & Hancock, 1983). The child who learns these social roles and responsibilities successfully is referred to as being *"bien educada"* (well-educated) (Zuniga, 1998, p 230 ; Saracho & Hancock, 1983)

Another aspect of adult-child interaction influenced by culture is the use of direct eye contact. In middle-class American culture, direct eye contact is expected, especially when speaking to someone. Although the speaker may shift eye contact periodically, the listener is expected to maintain steady eye contact as an indication that he or she is paying attention and is respectful. This pattern is quite different from most other cultures. Even in African American families where direct eye contact plays an important role, there are some interesting differences. For example, according to Adler (1993), in peer interactions, individuals may look directly at an individual while speaking but look away while listening. Also when there is a major difference in status, the individual may avoid eye contact as an indication of respect for authority. In addition, variations in eye gaze may be used to express nonverbal messages such as intimidation.

Among Asian American families, eye contact with authority figures is generally considered disrespectful (Chan, 1998; Cheng, 1987). Young children are not comfortable making eye contact with adults. Even among adults, direct eye contact is often inappropriate. For example, eye contact between males and females may have sexual connotations (Chan, 1998).

Nonverbal communications such as hand gestures and smiling may have different meanings and connotations in Asian-American families. For example, smiling may express embarrassment or apology in many southeast Asian groups (Chan, 1998). It can also express deference when being scolded by an authority, "thank you" in response to a compliment, or even mask negative emotions. In these cultures, smiling may express many things other than pleasure or joy.

Children's use of silence is often confusing for early childhood teachers. As will be discussed in more detail in the next chapter, mainstream United States culture values and encourages verbal assertiveness and competence. This is typically viewed as verbosity by other cultures. In many nonmainstream cultures, however, "silence is golden." This is especially true in many Asian cultures and in Native American tribal cultures. According to Cheng (1987), silence is often a sign of respect.

Physical contact is an area of adult-child interaction that is influenced by the children's home culture. Mexican American and African American children are comfortable with close proximity and being held or hugged. Mexican-American children and adults frequently make physical contact and maintain close physical proximity. Asian-American children are generally less comfortable with expressions of physical affection (although Asian girls often hold hands) (Cheng, 1989). Particularly noteworthy is the importance of avoiding touching the head of a Laotian child.(Cheng, 1989). Laotians believe that the "king of souls" resides in a person's head. The head is the most sacred part of the body and should not be touched.

Another cultural variant affecting the ways children interact with adults is the emphasis on autonomy and independence versus dependence and passivity. Middle-class children acquire a fair amount of independence by preschool age. Mastery of most self-help skills and some degree of decision-making and problem-solving also are expected. In many Asian families, however, while older children are strictly disciplined, parents tend to be very permissive with young children, and tend to view them as helpless. In some families, young children may be fed by parents until they are four years old and may not be allowed to play outside (Cheng, 1987). According to Ramirez (1989), in Mexican American families, parents tend to be fairly indulgent and protective of young children. Although there is a strong emphasis on the importance of good behavior, "there is a relaxed attitude toward the achievement of developmental milestones or the attainment of skills related to self-reliance" (p.228).

Unlike this emphasis on dependence in many Asian families, children from Native American tribal cultures develop independence at an early age. In many families, children experience the natural consequences (both social and physical) of their behaviors and choices. Sometimes, social service agencies and teachers view parents as neglectful because they endorse this early development of autonomy. A good example of a very nonmainstream way of dealing with children's behavior is provided by LaFromboise and Low (1989). The Hopi believe that as bad behaviors are repeated by a child, this accumulation of behaviors eventually leads to change. Therefore, parents may actually welcome repetitions of the negative behavior because it is a sign of imminent change for the better and they are reluctant to stop or change the behavior.

The teacher in a multicultural classroom must meet the needs of children who have greatly differing degrees of comfort in interacting with adults. Some children are extremely uncomfortable interacting with adults, while others interact easily, perhaps even aggressively. Some are highly independent and do not seek or welcome assistance and guidance from the teacher whereas others cling and seek attention. Still others are quietly withdrawn and appear relatively helpless and dependent. While these child characteristics are the result of many factors including child temperament, experience, family interaction patterns, and so on, culture plays an important role in determining how children interact with adults.

❖ PEER SOCIAL INTERACTIONS

Competition versus Cooperation

The ways in which young children play with each other are also influenced by their cultures. One of the obvious differences is in the area of competitiveness. An important value in United States culture is competition and individual achievement. Cooperation and altruism are not highly valued in mainstream culture. Cultural differences in cooperative versus competitive peer interactions probably are best documented in studies comparing Anglo and Mexican American children (McClintock, et al., 1983). A study of Mexican American and Anglo preschool children conducted by Knight & Kagan (1977) examined competitiveness in a beanbag throwing activity. The study concluded that the dominant motivation for Anglo preschool children was to *maximize* the differences between themselves and other children by outperforming them. Conversely, Mexican American children sought to *minimize* these differences. Cooperative children either avoid outperforming their peers or they help peers improve their own performance. Kagan (1983) describes three different types of social orientation.

1. "Cooperative" social orientation includes altruism (a preference for helping and protecting others), equality (a preference for equal outcomes), and group enhancement (seeking gains and avoiding losses for the group).
2. "Competitive" social orientation includes preferences for superiority (obtaining more than others) and rivalry (minimizing gains and maximizing losses of others).
3. "Individualistic" social orientation is a preference for obtaining gains and avoiding losses for *oneself.*

Competitive and individualistic social orientations are clearly dominant for most American mainstream children whereas for many nonmainstream groups (Mexican American and Native American tribes in particular) cooperation within the group and *avoidance* of "standing out" among ones peers are more characteristic.

By early school age, this orientation becomes deeply ingrained in a child's view of himself or herself and others. In a study by Chen, Rubin, & Sun (1992) two groups of children (Canadian and Chinese) were compared to determine what social characteristics were most associated with peer acceptance and rejection. This study found that the factor of "shyness and sensibility" was highly associated with peer acceptance among Chinese children but was associated with rejection among the Canadian children. In other words, in one culture, children who were highly sensitive and shy were regarded positively by their peers whereas in another culture, this characteristic was viewed negatively.

Kagan suggests that children's self esteem is influenced by the extent to which they achieve their culture's preferred social orientation. In other words, Anglo children do not feel good about themselves if they are not competitive, but Mexican American children's self-esteem is based on cooperativeness and altruism. Garcia (1983) points out that Mexican American children have less early exposure to peer groups than do Anglo children. Their early reference group is their siblings; and competition among siblings is not typically encouraged. Young mainstream children are more likely to experience group care at an earlier age and are already making social comparisons of one another by age three or four. According to Garcia (1983), Mexican American children do not become competitive until they have had several years of exposure to public school. Kagan (1983) suggests that United States classrooms, because of their competitive and individualistic social orientation, are biased against Mexican American children.

Although much of the research looked at cooperativeness and competitiveness in Mexican American children, this preference for cooperation and group rather than individual orientation is true of many other cultures as well. Among many Native American tribes, an emphasis on individual achievement is unacceptable (LaFromboise & Low, 1989). Children are taught to share and consider the good of family and community.

Kitano (1983) points out that because many Asian American cultures emphasize the importance of interdependency rather than individualism or competition, parents often teach cooperation to their children by stressing the effects of children's behavior on others. As children get older, however, there is a strong emphasis on individual academic achievement to bring honor to the family. Asian children, particular those from educated families, experience increasing pressures to achieve excellence in their school performance.

While competition is somewhat less emphasized in mainstream early childhood programs than was typical thirty years ago, there is still a strong emphasis on personal achievement as a key motivator. It is a challenge for middle-class early childhood professionals to find other ways to motivate children's participation. Appealing to the good of the group and the positive reflection on one's family are motivators that might be more effective with children from nonmainstream backgrounds than are appeals to individual performance and competition (Saracho & Hancock, 1983). For example, having two or three children draw together on a large sheet of paper instead of each making his or her own picture might be more inviting for some children. Talking about making something that a child's family would be proud of and could enjoy might be more of a motivation than simply asking the child to create a nice art project. As children get older, cooperative learning strategies can be used to encourage both cooperation and competition. For example, reward cooperative teams for team accomplishments. As teams compete with each other, success depends on the cooperation of each team member.

Play Styles

The ways in which young children play are not universal or simply related to innate maturational changes. Anthropological studies of play in different cultures around the world suggest that play styles are highly influenced by culture. Sutton-Smith and Roberts (1981) found that play is broadly categorized into three types:

1. Play that centers around physical self-testing such as jumping, throwing objects, developing strength, and manipulating small objects.

2. Play that imitates games and activities specifically modeled by older siblings or adults.
3. Symbolic play activities such as those characteristic of western cultures.

Symbolic play is typically highly verbal and creative, and is dependent on language. It is open-ended rather than rule-based or routinized.

Western style play also incorporates a variety of objects (blocks, legos, cars and trucks on tracks, dolls, and toy housekeeping items). Hale (1982) summarized the work of Ebsen who suggests that this object orientation actually interferes with the affective connections between mothers and infants. "In Western society objects come between the child and his mother. The babies are more prone to be bottle fed, carried around in baby carriages, placed in playpens to play alone, and placed in a separate bed for sleeping." (p. 58)

In the United States and Europe we are accustomed to thinking of symbolic and object play as universal and innate, that most developmental assessments, formal and informal, are based on this assumption. Child development literature is permeated with theories and studies of the stages of play development,

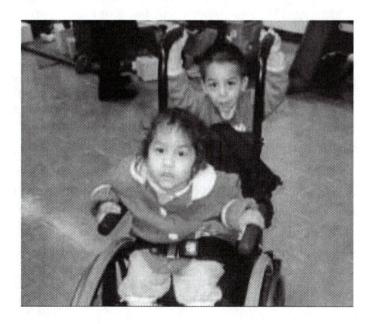

based primarily on observations of middle-class Anglo children (Roopnarine & Johnson, 1994).

It is important for early childhood professionals to understand not all children have been socialized to engage in symbolic or object play. For example, Hale (1983) points out that African American children are much more "feeling oriented, people oriented, and more proficient at nonverbal communication than White children" (p.23). Hale suggests that the characteristics of play reflect African influences. She tells of her attempts to study children's doll play in the African country of Ghana. She was informed that Ghanaian children don't play with dolls; they play with their mother's babies.

African American children often are raised in households where there are large numbers of individuals and ample opportunities for all kinds of interactions with emotionally expressive people. There may be little emphasis on toy play. In fact, an infant's physical exploration of an object is often redirected toward social interaction (Hale-Benson, 1986). For example, as the infant reaches for an object, the caregiver redirects the infant to pat her face.

As a result, a young African American child may be less object-oriented and less interested in manipulation and exploration of objects. Early childhood professionals from mainstream backgrounds erroneously judge this lack of physical exploratory behavior as an indication that the child is less curious or less bright than a typical middle-class child. In fact, an African American child may be much more sensitive to nonverbal interpersonal cues and more astute in judgments of adult emotions than are middle-class Anglo children.

Although many Asian children enjoy physical manipulation of objects, they may be less comfortable with open-ended symbolic play. Because Asian children are more comfortable when they know exactly what is expected of them, they find it difficult to be creative in play situations, especially those related to pretend social situations like, "Let's pretend I'm the mother and you're the baby and you won't take your nap," Pretend play of this type may be difficult for some children. Cheng (1987) suggests that Asian children may be less likely to engage in spontaneous interaction with peers or to participate in decision-making.

Stimulus Intensity

Early childhood professionals working in multicultural classrooms will be aware of differences in activity level and children's' needs for or tolerance of stimulus intensity. According to Hale (1982), frequent problems encountered by young black children are related to their high activity level and their preference for intense stimulation relative to Anglo children. African American children are typically used to active, emotionally intense social environments. They are often highly energetic, a quality sometimes referred to as "verve" (Hale-Benson, 1986) Black children may prefer spontaneous interactions. And they may find highly structured activities, with little variety and low intensity levels, boring. Unfortunately, these children—especially boys—are often labeled hyperactive or behavior disordered because of what may actually be a cultural mismatch (Hale, 1982, p.75). Also, African American children may be accustomed to more frequent snacks or meals as opposed to the typical middle-class schedule organized around three different meals. Therefore, the predictable schedules important to day care or preschool are unfamiliar to some children and require greater adjustment time.

Note that many Asian children may be at the opposite end of the continuum when it comes to tolerance for stimulus intensity and the need for routine schedules. Asian children may initially find the classroom much too noisy and chaotic, too open-ended, and not predictable enough!

Gender Differences

One of the greatest cultural variants in social behavior is the way in which gender roles are defined and the degree of difference between sociobehavioral expectations for men and women. These differences certainly are represented in children's early social development. Mainstream United States culture places a high value on equality of males and females, and early childhood educators try to eliminate gender bias and gender stereotyping from their curricula (see, for example, The Anti-bias Curriculum by Derman-Sparks, 1989). African American families also are less characterized by fixed gender roles as evidenced by the ease with which females assume head of household responsibilities and community leadership positions.

At the other end of the continuum are many cultures in which gender roles are very clearly defined and there is a reluctance to violate these roles. For example, in typical Asian and Latino families, males have higher status than females. In Latino culture, they learn to defend themselves and others when necessary. In Asian families, the males are the primary decision-makers and rule-makers. They are not challenged by their children or their spouse. Both Latina and Asian women are expected to be chaste and madonna-like, with a primary commitment to the home, raising children, and taking care of their spouses. Mexican American girls are often dressed in fancy dresses and are discouraged from engaging in messy play. Mexican American boys are often allowed to play vigorously and may be disciplined less often than girls. Similar gender role patterns are observed in families from Middle Eastern backgrounds

In many families, parents actively discourage little boys from playing with traditionally feminine toys such as dolls, dishes, and brooms. In such cases, boys may be reluctant to play with these materials at school. Similarly, girls may be reluctant to climb and engage in messy activities, or to defend themselves.

The challenge for the early childhood professional is to figure out ways to work toward the goals of the mainstream culture that include equal opportunity for boys and girls, and at the same time, respect families' values related to role differentiation.

❖ STRATEGIES FOR DEALING WITH DIFFERENCES IN CHILDREN'S SOCIAL SKILLS

The following are some suggestions for dealing with children's behaviors and interaction styles that may conflict with those of other children in the classroom or with the teachers' expectations for "normal" behavior.

1. Interact with children who need one-on-one attention in small groups. In small group settings, they get the adult attention they desire and gain experience interacting with peers.

2. If children do not express preferences or initiate an activity, provide the opportunity for a choice. Then, if the child does not choose, make the selection for the child. If there is an indication from the child that your selection was not his choice, cheerfully make the change and say, "I'm glad you let me know what you wanted." Be careful not to ignore the child who does not initiate or ask for what he or she needs. It is easy for these children to become invisible in large, heterogeneous classrooms.

3. Do not force children to make eye contact.

4. Do not pressure children to talk. Such pressure often backfires, resulting in even greater reluctance to talk. Provide many alternate means of expression, including art, music, puppets, signing, and so on.

5. If you as a teacher prefer to use first names, add a title such as "Miss Brigitte." This allows children to address the teacher with appropriate respect, important in many families (York, 1991).

6. For children who have had little experience separating from mothers, encourage mother to stay for the first part of the class. When she leaves,

have her say "good bye" instead of trying to sneak out without the child's noticing. If the child becomes upset at mother's leaving, hold and soothe the child. Ask mother for a transitional object such as a blanket or stuffed animal.

7. Keep plenty of large tee shirts on hand for children to wear over clothing during art activities and water play.

8. Provide ample opportunity for self-direction several times throughout the course of the day for children who are not used to schedules and routines (for example, at arrival time, free play time, and recess). Help the child learn the sequence of events in the daily routine.

9. If the child does not respond to positive discipline, use firm commands, at least initially. Gradually help the child comply with less direct forms of instructions. For example, help him or her realize that when the teacher says "Will everyone please clean up their art materials" that this actually means "You clean up now."

❖ DEVELOPMENT OF ETHNIC IDENTITY AND BIAS IN CHILDREN

The Cognitive Bases of Ethnic Identity and Prejudice

One key to dealing with the development of prejudice in young children is to understand that children's awareness of *differences*, and their generalizations about characteristics of groups, are normal cognitive processes whereas the development of negative attitudes toward these differences is not. A separate, but not unrelated process, is the development of ethnic or racial *identity*, the child's inclusion of ideas and attitudes toward his or her own ethnic or racial group into a private sense of self.

Children are aware of differences in individuals in infancy. For example, infants are able to tell the difference between primary caregivers and strangers. They are able to label and comment on the physical differences they observe sometimes as early as two years.

Sometimes three-year-olds show genuine discomfort in the presence of such differences. For example, the author's daughter once noticed a man who was completely bald and asked, "Why he hasn't got no hair?"

According to York (1991), the features most often commented on by children between two and five years are the following:

- features related to disabilities: wheelchairs, glasses, physical impairments, and special equipment
- features related to gender: male/female anatomy; girls comment on things they cannot do because they are not boys
- physical features: skin color, facial features, hair color, texture, and style
- cultural differences: language and accent; celebrations

As children become more verbal they begin to ask many "why" questions about these features: "Why is Tanya's hair like that?" Children also are confused about what characteristics change and what stays the same; for example, we grow taller, but our skin color stays the same. Children often believe skin color can be washed off (Derman-Sparks, 1989) or they hope to have different physical features when they grow up (York, 1991). Children need help sorting this out.

Ramsey (1987) discusses several cognitive processes involved in the development of children's thinking about ethnicity. The first is the process of categorization. The formation of categories is an important cognitive process that allows simplification of information by organizing a wide variety of facts into a limited number of classifications. As children organize information about differences between individuals, they create categories often based on racial and cultural characteristics. Initially, these categories are simple and center around a single defining feature. During the preschool years, it is difficult for children to understand there are many defining features of a group and that there often are exceptions to their own assumptions about the characteristics of a group. For example, a child who sees images of Native Americans consistently depicted on horseback with feathered headbands has a difficult time accepting someone in his class, dressed in shorts and tee shirt, as a Native American.

Children then absorb the beliefs and attitudes related to these groups most prevalent in the child's environment. By three years of age, children are observed imitating parent's prejudicial comments and behaviors. This input contributes in a very significant way to the development of children's prejudice. The following is a true example. A three and a-half-year-old white child refused to play with an African American peer. When the teacher asked him what was wrong, the child responded, "I don't like him. He's a gang."

Another cognitive process is the search for coherence. Children attempt to fit new information and experiences into their existing belief systems. Ramsey (1987) suggests that eventually, children resist information and experiences that challenge these beliefs. If the child's existing belief system includes mostly negative ideas about a particular group, this becomes a prejudice. Unfortunately, according to Ramsey, the child's natural process of searching for rules and consistency contributes to the stability of this belief system. In addition, as children learn the "rules" and characteristics that define their own world (styles of dress, ways of talking, food, odors, manners, and so on) traits in other children that do not conform to these expectations are automatically viewed as negative.

A study by Bigler and Leben (1993) examined the effect of children's level of cognitive development on their ability to remember "counter-stereotypical" information such as a story about an interracial friendship, an African American becoming a doctor, or a white boy singing rap music. Children's ability to remember counter-stereotypic traits was related to their ability to classify along multiple dimensions (the ability to reclassify a single individual as black, female, and a student). In addition, the more likely the child was to racially stereotype others, the poorer the child's memory was for counter-stereotypic information. In fact, information that did not fit children's stereotypes was not simply forgotten but often *distorted* to fit the child's existing prejudices.

What is clear is that the development of children's prejudice results from the interaction between the natural processes of cognitive development related to the formation of categories and search for rules and regularities in the world, as well as the child's absorption of negative attitudes toward certain categories or groups of people present in the child's social environment. What is also clear is that the prevention of prejudice in children requires active intervention on the part of significant adults in children's lives.

Awareness of Ethnic Identity

By the age of three, young children already are sensitive to differences in people's hair and skin color, and have a beginning awareness of ethnic groupings such as "black people" or "Chinese people". However, at this age, they are relatively unaware of their own ethnic affiliation (Rotheram & Phinney, 1987). Majority children are much less aware of their own ethnicity than are minority children (Rotheram & Phinney, 1987). Although Euro-American children do develop positive associations with, and preferences for, the color and label "white" (York, 1991), even though they do not necessarily refer to themselves as white.

Children's awareness of differences significantly increases between the ages of three to five years (Derman-Sparks 1989). According to Aboud (1988), it is during these years that children develop *attitudes* toward race and ethnicity. Because children's thinking at this age is simple and illogical, these attitudes often are based on one or two simple ideas or experiences.

The first evidences of prejudice most commonly noted are in the negative comments that three- to four-year-old white majority children make about non-white characteristics. During this period, it is also fairly common for minority children to make such negative comments about *themselves*.

Five- to six-year-old children become more group-oriented and begin to understand the concept of group membership. Children at this age are more likely to use language instead of physical acts to express aggression. As a result, there is a significant increase in name-calling at this age. "Bad names" for people often include racial or ethnic slurs. At the same time, however, as the complexity of children's thinking increases, they begin to have the capability to understand the problems with stereotypes and to grapple with what is "really real" and what is not. They are very rigid and rule bound. This is an advantage because children at this age have strict definitions of "fairness." This is an ideal developmental period to appeal to children's sense of fairness by pointing out the unfairness of discrimination; for example, not liking someone because of his or her skin color.

By age seven, children are well-aware that gender and skin color stay the same as they grow older. They understand that many of their own features come from their parents, and they are aware of their own ethnic identity. Cognitively, they use hierarchical thinking to understand they can be a member of several different groups simultaneously, such as a family, a classroom, an ethnic group, a religion, a city, at state, and so forth. As a result of the group affiliation, children at this age typically express preference for other children of their own race or ethnicity. Racial or ethnic identity is significantly stronger in minority children. According to King, Chipman, and Cruz-Janzen (1994), when white children are asked the question "Who are you?" they usually give their name. Minority children respond with their ethnicity such as "I'm an African American, much more often than will white children.

Between seven and nine years of age, children become much more aware of the world around them, of

things that happened in the past, and of what might happen in the future. This is a good developmental period in which to begin talking about the cultural history and heritage of different groups and of people from different countries.

Another critical cognitive achievement at this age is the ability to talk about feelings and to understand things from another person's perspective. This perspective-taking ability allows the development of empathy. During this stage, parents and teachers play a major role in rethinking and finalizing children's values and beliefs (York, 1991). According to Aboud (1988), after the age of nine, children's attitudes toward race are resistant to change. During the earlier preoperational phase, the limits on children's cognitive abilities make them vulnerable to societal and family influences on their attitudes toward differences. Teachers have a responsibility to mediate and limit these influences as much as possible during this developmental period. Then, once the child's thinking becomes better able to handle the complex issues of racial and ethnic identity, by age seven, he or she is able to develop ways of categorizing and understanding human diversity without prejudice.

Effects of Prejudice on Euro-American Children

According to York (1991), there is an initial denial of reality as parents attempt to discourage children's questions and comments about differences. Unfortunately, seeing parents' discomfort and being "hushed up" for noticing differences significantly interferes with children's understanding of differences. As a result, children deny these differences and believe that everyone is the same or that everyone is just like them.

Euro-American children learn very early that the customs and ways of doing things they are most familiar with are the best. This further enhances their negative emotional reaction to anything different. York goes on to suggest that to some extent, Euro-American children's self-esteem is tied to the belief that they are better than anyone else. If this is true, there is a natural tendency for white children to view who are different as inferior, in order to maintain their self-esteem.

Effects of Prejudice on Minority Children

Young minority children usually have positive attitudes toward white children. Minority children who attend preschool programs tend to prefer white dolls to dark colored dolls (Aboud 1988). By age five or six, minority children correctly identify their own ethnicity but often continue to prefer Euro-American characteristics. It is not until around age seven that minority children begin to prefer their own ethnic group and develop negative attitudes toward whites. Children do not become fully aware of their own group's social *status* until age eleven or twelve.

❖ STRATEGIES FOR PREVENTING THE DEVELOPMENT OF BIAS AND PREJUDICE IN YOUNG CHILDREN

Two excellent resources exist to assist early childhood professionals help young children deal with issues of racial and ethnic identity and prejudice. They are the *Anti-bias Curriculum: Tools for Empowering Young Children* (Derman-Sparks, 1989) and *Roots and Wings: Affirming Culture in Early Childhood Programs* (York, 1991). The section below uses these and other resources to give you some ideas regarding specific strategies. For additional ideas and explanations, refer directly to those sources.

Two general points must be kept in mind. The first is the importance of *valuing diversity*. This point is made so often we may fail to really connect with its meaning. Valuing diversity for young children means constantly pointing out how interesting and how positive differences are. Perhaps because of egalitarian, democratic values, mainstream Americans are generally uncomfortable with differences. "We are all the same" is a statement we think we should believe. There is a tendency to confuse equal opportunity with sameness. The right of equal opportunity and access does not mean everyone is alike. We need to find ways in the classroom to emphasize the concepts of sameness *and* difference. There is clearly a preference for "sameness" that runs throughout our educational system. Think of all the activities where children are reinforced for grouping together all the things that are alike, or for "finding the one that's different." How often after saying "Find the one that's different" do we go on to say "Find the one that *doesn't belong?*" The message is clear and repeated: "Different is bad."

Educational activities that require sorting and categorizing are not wrong. These are important cognitive skills absolutely essential to higher level analytical thinking, including math and language. Instead, the point here is that differences are also interesting and important. Being sensitive to differences in a positive way sharpens one's observation skills; provides more interest, variety, and excitement; and encourages artistic and emotional expression. Appreciating differences should not be limited to dealing with children's individual differences, but should be incorporated across the curriculum. For example, take children on walks and pick up leaves or stones and talk about how they are different. Read books and show pictures of different animals, and help children talk about how they differ from one another. Show different kinds of artwork or fabrics and ask the children how they differ from each other. The possibilities are simple and endless. It is easier to deal with children's observations of differences in their own physical characteristics by incorporating this interest in differences across all aspects of the curriculum.

The second key point is for early childhood professionals to acknowledge their own discomfort in dealing with children's ethnic and racial identity and bias. There is a tendency to ignore these issues, either in the hope they will go away, or because of the mistaken notion that bias and prejudice is made worse by paying attention to it. Children's concerns and attitudes about ethnic and racial differences are real and intense. You have a small window of opportunity to prevent these normal concerns and attitudes from becoming deeply ingrained prejudices that are invulnerable to change. If you cannot truly engage children and deal directly with this content, this opportunity is lost.

❖ TEACHER-CHILD INTERACTION STRATEGIES

Responding to Children's Comments about Differences

How adults respond to children's comments about differences or about experiences of discrimination is very important. Help children identify and verbalize their feelings. For example, if a child says "I don't like Julie because she's all dark," you need to do several things. According to York (1991), accurately acknowledge the observation of difference; for example, "Julie does have dark skin, just like her parents." Empathize with Julie's hurt feelings and help her express them: "It feels bad to have Tony say he doesn't like you because of the color of your skin, doesn't it Julie?" Without trying to make Tony feel guilty, remind the children there is a "bottom line" and that it is unacceptable and unfair to dislike someone because of skin color. As children get older, they will engage in dialogue around such episodes. This should be encouraged. Realize there will be tension and conflict around such topics. Children form their own ideas and attitudes based on family and media input. When this conflicts with what they learn at school, they may have great difficulty resolving this tension because of their cognitive limitations.

Examples of Specific Classroom Activities

Both York (1991) and Derman-Sparks (1989) describe a variety of specific early childhood activities to help children deal with issues of ethnic and racial identity and bias. Some of the suggested activities included here have been adapted from these authors. Note that while the focus of the activities is on acknowledging and valuing the uniqueness of each child, each activity is rich with opportunities for language and cognitive development, as well.

1. *Concept of Skin Color*. Have children mix white, yellow, brown, and red paint to try to match their

own skin colors. Talk about concepts of lighter and darker, as well as different color shades and hues such as golden brown, tan, peach, rosy pink, ivory, and so on.

2. *Body Image and Physical Differences.* Use a long piece of butcher paper and make a wall mural by tracing around each child. Have each child draw his or her own features and clothing styles. Put the mural on the wall and have the children identify each other. Ask how they know who the picture represents.

3. *Racial/Ethnic Constancy.* After a fingerpainting activity, demonstrate how paint washes off but skin color stays the same.

4. *Similarities and Differences.* Tape the children's voices. Have them listen and identify each other's voice. Talk about how voices are similar and different. Ask for two volunteers. Have them stand up and ask the other children to list all the ways they are similar and all the ways they are different. Start with clothing colors and styles, then hair color and style, and skin color and facial features. Keep emphasizing the theme "We are all alike and we are all different."

5. *Develop Social Sensitivity.* If a child is called names or discriminated against in some way, give that child a band aid. Allow him to talk about how the experience "hurts."

6. *Develop Empathy.* Make a clock face with a dial. In each of four quadrants draw faces expressing emotions of anger, sadness, happiness, and fear. Describe various situations, including examples of discrimination, and ask the children to turn the dial to the appropriate emotion.

7. *Develop Curiosity about Unfamiliar Customs.* At least once a week, have an activity called "Try It You'll Like It!" Bring in an unfamiliar food, game, or type of clothing. Encourage the children to try the experience and describe their reactions. Talk about how it takes time to enjoy unfamiliar things, and how if you don't try, you can miss out on something good. Encourage children and parents to contribute things from their own family and community.

Incorporating Antibias Strategies into All Aspects of the Curriculum

Both York (1991) and Derman-Sparks (1989) stress the importance of routinely integrating antibias and diversity awareness strategies into all early childhood activities. Some ways of doing this include the following:

1. Create a classroom culture that reflects all its diversity by keeping an ongoing scrapbook with the children's photos, art projects, and souvenirs from key events throughout the year.
2. Make sure art materials reflect all skin and hair colors.
3. Frequently refer to the colors brown and black in positive ways such as "The horse in this story has a very beautiful black mane." Counteract as best you can the almost universal notion that "white is good" and "black is bad."
4. Increase the number of brown and black manipulatives. If necessary, paint some blocks and shape pieces brown and black.
5. Eliminate books and toys that reinforce stereotypes.
6. Include representations of racial and ethnic groups in storybooks and dolls.
7. Provide clothing and work props that reflect all kinds of male and female roles in the dramatic play area such as beautician, custodian, bus driver, homemaker, store clerk, and so on.
8. Introduce key words in different languages such as, The word for "yellow" in Spanish is "amarillo." Include key vocabulary in sign language: this enables children to learn there are many different languages. Sing songs in English and another language (ask parents to help with translations).
9. Reinforce knowledge of more than one language.
10. Find ways to demonstrate and value similarities and differences throughout all aspects of the curriculum. Avoid the association that being different is bad, or if it's different, it "doesn't belong."

❖ REFERENCES

Adler, S. (1993). *Multicultural communication skills in the classroom*. Boston: Allyn and Bacon.

Allen, L., & Majidi-Ahi, S. (1989). Black-American children. In J. T. Gibbs & L. N. Huang (eds.), *Children of color* (pp. 148–178). San Francisco: Jossey-Bass Publishers .

Aboud, F. (1988). *Children and prejudice.* New York: Basil Blackwell.

Bigler, R. A., & Leben, L. S. (1993). A cognitive-developmental approach to racial stereotyping and reconstructive memory in Euro-American children. *Child Development, 64*(5), 1507–1518.

Chan, S. (1998). Families with Asian roots. In M. Hanson & E. Lynch (eds.), *Developing cross-cultural competence: A guide for working with young children and their families* 2nd ed. (pp. 251–347). Baltimore: Paul H. Brookes Publishing.

Chen, X., Rubin, K. H., & Sun, Y. (1992). Social reputation and peer relationships in Chinese and Canadian children: A cross-cultural study. *Child Development, 63*(6), 1336–1343.

Cheng, L. L., (1987). *Assessing Asian language performance.* San Diego: Aspen Publications.

Derman-Sparks. L. (1989). *Anti-bias curriculum: Tools for empowering young children.* Washington DC: National Association for Young Children.

Garcia, E. E. (Ed.). (1983).*The Mexican-American child: Language, cognition and social development.* Tempe, AZ: Arizona State University: Center for Bilingual Education.

Hale, J. E. (1982). Black children: Their roots, culture and learning style. Provo, UT: Brigham Young University Press.

Hale, J. E. (1983). Black children: In O. Saracho & B. Spodek (eds), *Understanding the multicultural experience in early childhood education.* Washington, DC: NAEYC.

Hale-Benson, J. E. (1986). *Black children: Their roots, culture and learning style.* (rev. ed.) Baltimore: Johns Hopkins University Press.

Huang, L. H., & Ying, Y. (1989). Chinese-American children and adolescents. In J. T. Gibbs & L. N. Huang (eds.), *Children of color* (pp. 30–66). San Francisco: Jossey-Bass Publishers.

Kagan, S. (1983). Social orientation among Mexican American children: A challenge to traditional classroom structures. In E. E. Garcia (ed.), *The Mexican-American child: Language, cognition and social development* (pp. 163–182). Tempe, AZ: Arizona State University: Center for Bilingual Education.

King, E., Chipman, M., & Cruz-Janzen, J. (1994) *Educating young children in a diverse society.* Boston: Allyn & Bacon.

Kitano, M. (1983). Early education for Asian-American children. In O. N. Saracho & B. Spodek, (eds.), *Understanding the multicultural experience in early childhood education* (pp. 45–66). Washington, DC: National Association for Education of Young Children .

Knight, G. P., & Kagan, S. (1977). Development of prosocial and competitive behaviors in Anglo American and Mexican American children. *Journal of Cross-Cultural Psychology*, 48, 1385–1394.

LaFromboise, T. D., & Low, K. G. (1989). American Indian children and adolescents. In J. T. Gibbs & L. N. Huang (eds.), *Children of color* (pp. 114–147). San Francisco: Jossey-Bass Publishers.

McClintock, E., Bayard, M. P., & McClintock, C. G. (1983). The socialization of social motivation in Mexican-American families. In E. E. Garcia (ed.) *The Mexican-American child: Language, cognition and social development* (pp. 143–162). Tempe, AZ: Arizona State University: Center for Bilingual Education.

Nagata, D. (1989). Japanese American children and adolescents. In J. T. Gibbs & L. N. Huang (eds.), *Children of color* (pp. 67–113). San Francisco: Jossey-Bass Publishers.

Ramirez, O. (1989). Mexican American children and adolescents. In J. T. Gibbs & L. N. Huang (eds.), *Children of color* (pp. 224–250). San Francisco: Jossey-Bass.

Ramsey, P. (1987) Young children's thinking about ethnic differences. In J. S. Phinney & M. J. Rotheram (eds.), *Children's ethnic socialization*. Beverly Hills, CA: Sage Publications.

Rotheram, M. J., & Phinney, J. S. (1987). Introduction: Definitions and perspectives in the study of children's ethnic socialization. In J. S. Phinney & M. J. Rotheram (eds.), *Children's ethnic socialization*. Beverly Hills: Sage Publications.

Roopnarine, J. L., & Johnson, J. E., (1994). The need to look at play in diverse cultural settings. In J. L. Roopnarine, J. E. Johnson, & F. H. Hooper (eds), *Children's play in diverse cultures* (pp. 1–8). Albany: State University of New York Press.

Saracho, O. N., & Hancock, F. M. (1983). Mexican-American culture. In O. N. Saracho & B. Spodek (eds.), *Understanding the multicultural experience in early childhood education* (pp. 3–16). Washington DC: National Association for Education of Young Children.

Sutton-Smith, B., & Roberts, J. M. (1981). Play, games and sports. In H. C. Triandis & A. Heron (eds.), *Handbook of cross-cultural psychology: Developmental Psychology* Vol. 4 (pp. 425–471). Boston: Allyn & Bacon.

Young, V. H. (1970). Family and childhood in a Southern Georgia community. *American Anthropologist, 72,* 269–288.

York, S. (1991). Roots and wings. Affirming culture in early childhood programs. St. Paul, MN: Redleaf Press.

Zigler, E., Abelson, W., & Seitz, V. (1973). Motivational factors in the performance of economically disadvantaged children on the Peabody Picture Vocabulary Test. *Child Development, 44*(2), 294–303.

Zuniga, M. E. (1998). Families with Latino roots. In M. Hanson & E. Lynch (eds.), *Developing cross-cultural competence: A guide for working with young children and their families* (2nd ed.) (pp. 209–250). Baltimore: Paul H. Brookes Publishing.

Chapter 5

Cultural Influences on Communication Skills and Styles

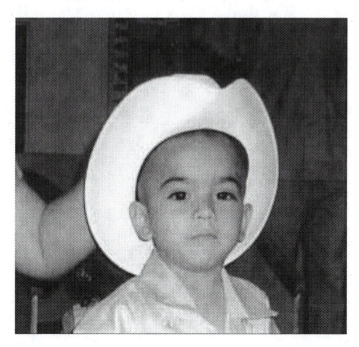

There is probably no single curriculum area as important to school and social success as the development of communication skills. Consider the following well-established points:

- communication skills provide the foundation on which the literacy skills of reading and writing develop;
- the ability to use language effectively in different situations and for different purposes is crucial to the development of social skills;
- the development of communication skills depends on the kind of early adult-child interaction experienced by young children; and
- the ways in which language is learned, used, and spoken is determined by culture and varies significantly among cultures.

As an early childhood professional working with young children, you will find that language and communication skills are not only crucial to children's development but also are vulnerable to environmental influences. More specifically, these influences begin with cultural traditions and the linguistic environment. The linguistic environment includes the specific language and dialect spoken such as Castilian Spanish, Standard American English, or Black English. Cultural traditions determine how language is *used*. For example, many Native Americans use language to maintain an oral tradition of storytelling. Some middle-class families develop aggressive uses of language (such as arguing) as a means of establishing dominance and independence. These patterns and styles of communication are then transmitted to children by adults and older children.

It is important that teachers of young children realize these influences come not only from children's families and communities but also from the child care center and classroom. Often, the linguistic and social communication patterns experienced by middle-class children in middle-class communities are similar across all environments. In other words, the language and communication patterns used in children's homes are similar to the expectations and goals for language use in the classroom. There is a perfect match. However, as we see in this chapter, and as was discussed briefly in

Chapter 4, for nonmainstream, culturally different families, this is not always the case. When there is a mismatch between the home and school with regard to spoken language and the ways it is used, the development of important language foundations for literacy, school achievement, and social skills are impeded (Iglesias, 1985b).

As an early childhood professional, it is important that you understand the nature of such mismatches and develop the skills necessary to turn children's different communicative backgrounds and experiences into advantages rather than disadvantages. The skilled educator can learn to prevent the potential adverse effects of cultural difference on social and academic achievement.

❖ ADULT-CHILD INTERACTION

In the previous chapter, we discussed some of the characteristics of child-rearing practices that vary in interesting ways across cultures. We also stressed the point that child-rearing practices are not "good" or "bad," but simply different. However, certain child-rearing practices "match" more closely the expectations of mainstream culture. Subsequently, these practices produce children whose behaviors match the expectations of the schools in which they perform and achieve.

The kinds of child-rearing practices that have the greatest influence on the development of children's language skills are parent-child interactions. Many studies show that how parents talk to their children, and how they respond to children's communicative attempts, have significant effects on the development of language (Gottfried, 1984; Dellacorte, Benedict, & Klein, 1983).

Verbal and Nonverbal Interactions

One way in which caregivers vary in their interactions with young children (particularly infants) is in their use of vocal (sounds) and verbal (words and sentences) interaction. For example, some Native Americans, although very sensitive to their infants' cues, are verbally unresponsive. They are more likely to respond by touching the baby or shifting his or her position than vocalizing or talking (Westby, 1985). Some parents from lower socioeconomic backgrounds believe it is senseless to talk to infants before they understand what is said (Heath, 1983) On the other hand, middle-class caregivers in the United States and Europe are notorious for talking to even the youngest infant and carrying on lengthy "conversations" long before the infant demonstrates speech or comprehension.

Responsivity

Probably no caregiver behavior has a greater impact on all aspects of development than responsivity to child cues. Whether parents frequently respond to their young children's vocal/verbal behavior is highly variable. Some caregivers respond to an infant or toddler's motor behavior or facial expression, not to a sound or word. For example, one mother is responsive to her infant's waving arms; she smiles and waves back at the baby, or jiggles him on her knee. However, she may not notice when the baby makes babbling noises. Another mother may not pay attention to the arm-waving, but when the infant babbles or coos, she may respond by imitating the baby's sounds or move closer to the baby's face and say something like "Are you talking to Mama?"

Use of Repetition and Expansion

As babies get older, middle-class caregivers become linguistically fine-tuned to their children's experiences (Cross,1984). They "map" language onto whatever the child is experiencing at the time. For example, a young child notices an interesting colored stone in the grass and tries to pick it up. Although many mothers help the child pick up the stone, the middle-class mother (or father) accompanies this task with a great litany of verbal description:

MOTHER	CHILD
"Oh you see a stone don't you!	
You want me to help you get the stone?	"Stone!"
It's a very pretty stone.	
It's red. It's a red stone!	
There, you've got the stone."	

To caregivers from many cultures, the parents in this example seem excessively verbose. Nevertheless, the example contains many strategies documented as important in developing the kind of cognitive and linguistic skills that prepare children for success in mainstream public schools:

1. *Repetition.* Repetition of key words and phrases appears to be important in helping children learn language. Indeed, it is a key principle of learning for children and adults. In the sample above, the word "stone" is used five times. The word "red" is used twice.
2. *Recasting.* Recasting is related to repetition in that it involves restating ones own words and sentences in slightly different ways. For example, Mother says "It's red", followed by, "It's a red stone." Although redundant, it is not an exact repetition of the first sentence. The sentence is "recast" into a similar but slightly different sentence.
3. *Expansion.* Expansion involves taking the word the child says and expanding it into a longer sentence. In the example above, when the child says "stone," mother puts it in a sentence and says, "It's a very pretty stone." Expansion also involves adding a bit more information to what the child said such as adding the words "pretty" and "red." This is called *semantic extension.*

Referential Language

Also important to later school success is the use of *referential language.* Referential language is critical to the later development of literacy skills and is characterized by using the specific names of things and actions instead of using general or nonspecific language. In the example above, the child is more likely to learn the words "stone," "pretty," and "red" than if his mother had said, "Oh, what is that? Let me help you. OOh look! There it is! Now you have it don't you!"

This simple linguistic difference can make a big difference in the development of vocabulary, and of clear and precise thinking and communication. However, it is not a natural style of communication for everyone. In many cultures, if a thing is obvious, it is not named. For example, a rural Mexican mother can teach her daughter to make tortillas through demonstration and assistance. She may use very little language. There is a "shared reference" and the meaning is clear. In such cultures, because communication with children is typically concrete and the topics of conversation are present and visible, it may not seem necessary or even appropriate to use referential language in this context (Heath, 1986).

On the other hand, in some families, this referential use of labels comes naturally. A study of early language development by Roger Brown (1973) described the "Naming Game" that he believed to be a typical pattern of parent-child interaction in the families he studied. Visit any middle-class suburb in the United States and the naming game is observed readily: at the zoo, in the grocery store, riding on the freeway, or cooking dinner. However, it is important to realize that this verbal behavior, so common and closely related to children's development of vocabulary, may be uncommon or even viewed as bizarre by parents of other cultures.

A recent study compared the spontaneous language used by African American and white mothers while looking at story books with their two-year-old children (Haynes & Saunders, 1999). All mothers were from middle-class socioeconomic backgrounds (thereby controlling for class differences). Although there were few differences between the two groups in their language styles during this activity, a significant difference occurred in the use of labels; white mothers used many more labels than did African American mothers (an average of 20 versus 6 labels per episode).

❖ LANGUAGE FUNCTIONS

Obviously, these adult-child interaction patterns influence how children themselves use language (the purposes for which language is used). In mainstream cultures in most industrialized societies, verbal competence and verbal aggressiveness are valued (Westby 1985). Children learn to be clear and specific, use language in precise ways, describe and narrate on request, and argue logically and provide explanations. It is not uncommon for middle-class parents to "give in" to very young children's requests or protests if presented logically and convincingly. Children are conversational partners with adults at a very young age.

In many other cultures, however, such verbal behavior is discouraged and considered inappropriate for young children. Children learn by listening and observing adults' behaviors and actions (Crago, 1992). In many traditional Asian families, children may not initiate conversation with an adult or challenge the directives of those in authority.

In many cultures, the focus of adult-child interactions is more upon social uses of language instead of on learning language for its own sake. For example, in Mexican American families, very young children take part in a "triadic" interaction among child, parent, and another adult (Eisenberg, 1982). The child is told to "Tell Grandma 'Thank-you for the beautiful barettes'," or Tell Aunt Maria you 'had a very nice time at the party'." In this way, the child learns words and sentences as he or she becomes socialized into appropriate social/interpersonal practices.

Heath and others (Heath, 1983; Ochs, 1982; Schieffelin, 1990) described cultures where children learn language primarily by being present during adult conversation instead of through parent-child interaction (American Samoans and rural black communities). In these cultures, children learn language by imitating the ends of adult sentences or imitating the stressed part of adult sentences. As children imitate pieces of adults sentences, they attract the attention of adults who then include them in conversations. This language acquisition process is different from middle-class practices because the child must demonstrate some language ability before adult-child interaction begins to play an important role.

In many Native American cultures, language occurs primarily within the context of work and learning important crafts. For example, as young boys help with woodworking activities, they learn the names of tools and materials.

❖ CHILDREN'S USE OF NARRATIVE IN DIFFERENT CULTURES

Social anthropologist Shirley Brice Heath reported interesting studies of differences in young children's uses of language. Heath studied children's early language development and parent-child communicative interaction in several cultures, and described children's use of different types of narratives, or "narrative genres."he identifies four major types of narrative: recounts, eventcasts, accounts, and stories (Heath, 1986).

Recounts

The use of recounts is very common in mainstream cultures. Adults ask children to describe or narrate something that happened. Often, an adult who already knows the events asks the child to narrate the events to someone else. Children narrate on cue, and must learn to describe events with language that is clear and well-sequenced. For example, a mother may say to a young child, "Tell daddy what we did today." The child recites the experiences of a birthday party or a trip to grandmother's house. This kind of of narration is typical of the preschool and kindergarten classroom "show and tell" and "circle time" activities where children describe what they did on the weekend. Later, children write such narrations in their early essays such as "What I did on Christmas Vacation." According to Heath, recounts are common in middle-class families and in American schools but they are relatively uncommon in nonmainstream cultures.

Eventcasts

Another type of narrative, typical in mainstream cultures but very unusual in nonmainstream families, is called eventcasts. An eventcast is an immediate description of an ongoing event or the labeling of something obvious. For example, a mother observes her son coloring in a coloring book and asks, "What are you doing, Jon?" Despite the fact it is obvious what the child is doing, she asks him to describe, or narrate, his ongoing action. The use of language to describe the obvious is quite unusual in most cultures. It is, however, a common expectation in preschool and early elementary classrooms. Frequently, teachers ask children to describe their art activity, or objects and events in a picture. Many children find this a strange use of language because they must explain something that is obvious to the teacher. Because describing the obvious is considered disrespectful to the adult in some cultures (Heath, 1983), this can create discomfort for the child.

The potential for mismatch between the home and the classroom in terms of cultural expectations for language use is clearly demonstrated in recounts and eventcasts.

Accounts

Accounts are similar to recounts, but with one major difference. While recounts are a recitation requested by an adult, accounts are spontaneous narrations initiated by the child. Accounts are a genuine sharing of interesting or important past events. Children learn how to initiate these accounts in appropriate ways. They often begin with "Hey, ya know what . . ." or "Guess what happened . . . ." According to Heath, children's use of accounts is common in many cultures. Unfortunately, this type of narrative is not as acceptable in school environments. Although tolerated at the preschool level, as children get older, the use of accounts becomes less acceptable. Such child-initiated communication is viewed as an interruption or off-task if not occurring in response to a teacher cue or regularly scheduled classroom activity.

Stories

Perhaps the most common form of narrative in most cultures (except middle-class mainstream culture) is the story. Stories are descriptions of historical events.

Often, they are handed down in families or communities for generations. However, they also may evolve over a few years in a child's lifetime. Stories are told over and over and often undergo transformations and elaborations with time. They are a mixture of truth and fiction and are "performed" in the sense they include audience participation and props. When stories are handed down from generation to generation, they represent an important part of a community or family's cultural heritage. Stories that develop within a shorter time span often begin with a comical or dramatic event about which someone is teased by older members of the community or family. Over the years as the story is repeated about the individual, it becomes an important part of his or her identity. For many cultures, storytelling is one of the most important uses of language. For example, it plays an important part in the social-communicative interactions in Mexican American (Saracho & Hancock 1983), Native American (Tafoya, 1983), Appalachian Black (Heath, 1983), and Asian (Cheng, 1987) families. In middle-class families in the United States , however, storytelling is relatively uncommon. It is also virtually nonexistent in the classroom. Although true that teachers read books to children, it is a different kind of storytelling event. Pictures are unfamiliar, the story events do not relate to children's lives, and there is little opportunity for the children to retell the stories themselves or to elaborate on the story.

Gutierrez-Clellen and Quinn (1993) summarize the differences in narratives across cultures. They point out that the narratives of European-American children are typically detailed, structured, and chronological (linear). Cheng (1997) points out that some Asian discourse patterns are circular and provide extensive information, but they are without a topic statement or conclusion. The narratives of African American children are described as "episodic," often move from event to event, and contain many statements of judgement about the characters. One of the most frequently described studies of narrative style is of native Hawaiian children in the Kamehameha Early Education Project (Au & Jordan, 1981; Peregoy & Boyle, 1993) Their narrative styles differ significantly from the linear, sequential style of mainstream children, and make use of props and actions within their stories.

Another area of difference relates to the relative importance of nonverbal cues in communication. For example, African Americans tend to place great emphasis on nonverbal expression such as gestures, posture, body movements, nonverbal sounds, and intonations. Indeed, it is these nonverbal features that give the communication style of many African Americans its great appeal.

❖ CULTURAL INFLUENCES ON CLASSROOM COMMUNICATION

The information presented above provides some understanding into how the child-care or preschool classroom situation can create a very foreign and unusual communicative environment for the young child. As mentioned in earlier chapters, structured group-care environments and classrooms are often very new and different experiences for children from nonmainstream environments. They may not have attended Sunday School classes, play groups, ""Mommy-and-Me" classes, Gymboree, or ballet classes, the early experiences that prepare middle-class children for the classroom from an early age. In some cases, children may enter a preschool program without ever having been away from parents, or having been cared for by anyone other than a close and familiar relative.

Young children's willingness to talk—regardless of their cultural background—depends on their social context. One of the authors of this text recalls an experience with her daughter, Erin. At 18 months, she was very talkative and impressed her parents with her verbal precociousness. However, the regular babysitter, who had two very active older boys in the home, commented she was concerned because Erin had not started to talk! Erin was an only child; the culture in her home was different from that of the babysitter's. Erin's communicative behavior differed greatly in the two environments. Similarly, a study by Lein (1978) found that young migrant children who were verbally competent at home spoke almost exclusively in monosyllables in the classroom.

Young children from nonmainstream cultures often maintain a period of silence in the classroom for an extended period of time. It is important to respect this silence. Do not pressure children to talk. Instead, give them opportunities to talk within the natural contexts of their daily activities. This topic will be discussed further in later sections.

Another important area of cultural difference relates to when, how, and whether young children communicate with adults. In a few cultures, there is little verbal interaction between adults and young children. For example, this was found to be true in a study of young Samoan children (Ochs, 1982). Most of the language modeling is provided by older siblings. Some cultures do not encourage children to initiate communication. This was characteristic of many mainstream American families earlier in our history. Children were told "not to speak unless spoken to." In many cultures, when children do speak to adults, there are important rules which govern how to do so in a respectful manner. For example, several Native American groups do not condone direct eye contact between young children and authority figures. Many languages (for example, Lao and Japanese) require the use of certain grammatical "polite forms" such as different forms of pronouns when addressing persons of different status (Cheng, 1987).

In addition to cultural influences on whether a child talks at all, and on how comfortable a child is talking to adults, "school language" has many rules and characteristics that are confusing or uncomfortable for nonmainstream children (Tattershall & Creaghead, 1985).

One that we discussed at some length is talking about the obvious, what Heath calls "eventcasts" (Heath, 1986). Much of our early childhood school culture incorporates this particular type of language use. Children frequently talk about pictures, activities, and objects present or happening at the moment. For example, the following questions are typical:

While a child observes a pet gerbil eating, the teacher asks, "What's the gerbil doing?"
While the child is coloring, the teacher asks, "What are you doing, Laura?"
While looking at a book, the teacher asks, "Who can tell us what's happening in this picture?"

Such questioning prepares students for success as they enter elementary school where the modus operandi for formal teacher-student interaction is the "test question format" (Mehan 1979). In the test question format, the teacher asks questions related to content, such as reading and math, to check students' knowledge and attention. These are not real questions because the teacher already knows the answer; she is not really seeking information from the student; rather she is testing the student's knowledge. It is important to realize that many young children find such questioning regarding the obvious unusual. For example, Heath (1983) points out that in the black community she studied, talking about something obvious in the immediate context was considered inappropriate. A study by Pena and Quinn (1997) reported that African American and Latino American preschool children as a group performed poorly on a test that required labeling of pictures, and that the test could not discriminate between typically developing children and those with language delays. On the other hand, a test that involved describing functions of objects—a task with which children were more familiar—accurately discriminated between children with language delay and children whose language development was within normal limits.

There is a directness in United States culture quite unlike most other cultures of the world. Americans "tell it like it is" and value precise, explicit, direct communication. This is not the case in many other cultures. For example, Lemlech (1977) points out that the Spanish language is somewhat protective of the speaker. She cites Olguin's (1968) example of someone asking a child to explain who broke the dish. The child might respond "It fell from my hand." In mainstream settings, such a response is considered vague or indicative of the child's unwillingness to accept responsibility. Hale (1982) points out that one West African influence on the communication of African Americans is the value placed on circumlocution and paraphrase, instead of on direct statements and definitions. A direct and succinct language style is considered crude and inelegant. Cheng (1987) points out that Asian children are not comfortable speaking directly to adults and rarely say "no" for fear of hurting the teacher's feelings.

In our discussion of narrative genres, we discussed more common uses of language: telling familiar stories or giving accounts or explanations of events unknown to the listener. Some children become comfortable talking about pictures in a book only after those pictures become a well-established prop for a familiar story, one told so many times before that it has become part of the culture of the classroom. Or a child may not be willing to explain what he is drawing, but is much more willing to explain how someone was hurt on the playground because the bicycle pedal came off.

In addition to stories and explanations, there are some other uses of language with which young children may be quite comfortable. For example:

- using language to request things wanted or needed;
- using language to regulate and control other children's behavior;
- using language to entertain and joke; and
- using language to express frustration and negative emotions.

These uses, though common, are different from the most common uses of language in classrooms.

Iglesias (1985b) made the point that American schools are designed specifically to promulgate and support United States culture . The point we make here is that we groom children from the dominant culture from infancy to perform according to the cultural norm in public school classrooms. Preschools and other early education programs are important steps along the way in this preparation. Young children, whose early experiences with language have been *different* (in the ways we have been describing in this chapter), may not be as successful in preschool, may not find it to be a positive experience, and subsequently experience less positive success in the early primary grades.

❖ CHILDREN FROM NON-ENGLISH SPEAKING BACKGROUNDS

The most obvious cultural influence on communication is the native language spoken in the home. Today, many early childhood programs include a large proportion of children who do not speak English or who have a limited command of the English language. The NAEYC position statement (1996) on linguistic and cultural diversity acknowledges the importance of maintaining the child's home language, and, at the same time, creating learning environments that support the development of English

As a result of the work of individuals like Jim Cummins (1984) and Stephen Krashen (1981, 1992), we have a much better understanding of the processes of second language acquisition. It also is clear that there are cognitive advantages to becoming proficient in more than one language (Hakuta & Garcia, 1989).

Perhaps the most important thing for the early childhood professional to understand is that for children learning a second language, it is much like learning a first language. The stages children go through are similar to the stages of learning their native language (Krashen, 1981) Learning a second language is best accomplished within the context of interesting and meaningful activities when the language heard is simple, and matches what the child experiences at the time. Strategies such as repetition, redundancy, expansion and recasting sentences, and use of referential language—all discussed earlier in this chapter—are as important for second language acquisition as they are for first language acquisition.

In the early childhood classroom or day-care center children represent a wide variety of different stages of both first and second language acquisition. Some children are in the process of learning two languages simultaneously: their native language and English. Current evidence suggests that, for normally developing children, learning two languages is not necessarily more difficult than learning one *if the learning environments are responsive and consistent.* It is also the case, however, that if a child has difficulty learning the first language, he or she will have difficulty learning the second language. This also is true for preschool children who mastered their first language (typically by age three or four) and then must learn English as a second language. The ease with which children learn a second language is based to a great extent on their competence in their first language (Krashen, 1992). A solid foundation of skill in the first language greatly assists learning a second language.

Therefore, there is great variability among children in the early childhood setting. Many young children learn their native language and English simultaneously; other, somewhat older children—particularly if they have not attended early childhood programs previously—are learning English as a second language. The greater variability, however, may not result from the amount of exposure to and competence in English, but from the kind of communicative environments to which they are exposed, both at home and in the early childhood setting. As discussed previously, certain kinds of environments greatly facilitate the development of language competence.

Stages of Second Language Acquisition

According to Cummins (1984), it typically takes about two years from the time of first exposure for a child to learn a second language well enough to carry on social communication. This kind of proficiency is referred to as "basic interpersonal communication skill" (BICS). However, Cummins also points out that it takes much longer—as many as seven years—to learn a language well enough to function academically. This type of proficiency is called "cognitive academic language proficiency" (CALP). Teachers often overestimate children's English language proficiency. It is easy to assume that because a child makes simple requests and functions socially, that he mastered the language. Be aware of major gaps in language comprehension—particularly when there are few visual cues relating to the topic—in vocabulary and complex sentence construction.

The stages of second language acquisition are similar to the stages of first language acquisition (Tabors, 1997). These are summarized below:

The Silent Period. Depending on temperament, many children do not talk as they learn English. They achieve some level of comprehension (in familiar contexts) and they know a few words, but many children do not speak at all during this period. Outgoing and impulsive children speak more readily during this early stage.

Single Words and Early Word Combinations. During the next stage, children use single words and simple two- and three-word combinations. The child learns the most important words in the sentence and leaves out less critical words such as auxiliary verbs ("is," "are," "were") or prepositions ("on" or "to"). A typical utterance at this stage is "Bathroom!" or "Jorge go car."

Depending on the grammar of their native language, children may misorder words during this stage. For example, Spanish frequently places the adjective after the noun, (perro rojo) whereas English always places the adjective before the noun (the red dog). Because of this major grammatical difference, early utterances of some children learning English reflect this ("the dog red"). Again, depending on temperament, some children are reluctant to speak at this stage.

Simple Sentences with Grammatical Errors. Once children reach a stage where they can produce simple sentences of the form Subject-Verb-Object (e.g., "Jason hit me" or "Me bring a sandwich"), they begin to gain social competence in the new language. At this stage, they convey most simple ideas, particularly in context. Many grammatical errors continue for some time to come as children struggle to master the arbitrary and somewhat inconsistent rules of English grammar. These include words endings such as past tense ("ed"), present progressive ("ing"), plural and possessive ("s"), and so on. Auxiliary verbs are particularly troublesome in the English language including "is," "are," "have," "been," and "will," and pronoun forms such as "I," "me," "you," "he," "him," "his," and "her."

Social Fluency. At this stage, children handle most social situations and sound fairly fluent although some grammatical errors persist. They also master more complex forms of sentence structure such as "I had to go to my grandma's because my mom went to have a new baby." Despite this level of competence, however, there is still much they cannot understand or say. Their social fluency at this stage is deceptive.

Cognitive/Academic Language Proficiency. It takes approximately seven years to acquire sufficient language proficiency to understand and express the kinds of language associated with academic achievement. The conceptual, hierarchical, and analytical thinking required in content areas such as mathematics, literature, science, and economics requires the highest level of language fluency.

Rate of Language Acquisition in Bilingual Children

Because there are few longitudinal studies of the language development of bilingual children, detailed descriptions of the typical language development patterns of children raised bilingually are not available. According to Genesee and Nicoladis (1995), the stages and ages of major milestones of language structure (e.g., first words, word combinations, sentences, and so on) are similar for monolingual and bilingual children. However, there does appear to be a slower rate of vocabulary development for bilingual children when compared to monolingual children.

Dialect Differences

It is important to comment at least briefly on dialect differences. Many children speak English, but they speak a dialectal variation that interferes with their ability to comprehend and feel comfortable with the Standard American Dialect which is often used in early childhood settings.

We speak many dialects in the United States. We are familiar with Southern dialects, dialects from the boroughs of New York City, the New England dialect, and Black Dialect. The American dialect receiving the most attention and formal study is Black English Dialect. Many (although not all) African Americans speak this dialect, or some form of it. It differs from Standard American Dialect in several interesting ways. The "phonology" or sound system is different. Words are pronounced differently, and there is a more melodic speech quality. The grammar of Black Dialect is also different in the use of "to be" verbs and the omission of tense markers such as past tense "ed". Finally, there are significant regional differences in vocabulary, including words that do not exist in Standard Dialect (for example, the word "dis" meaning to insult or disrespect as in "Don't dis me!"), and different meanings of words (for example, the word "attitude" meaning "bad attitude"). Hale (1982, p. 64) points out that Black English serves as an important vehicle for cultural cohesion and identity. Many of the challenges that exist for children from non-English speaking homes as they attempt to learn English as a second language also exist for children who speak different dialects. In the 1970s, Lemlech (1977) and others advocated teaching English as a second language to speakers of Black Dialect.

It is critical that teachers respect children's language dialects. Because Black English is associated with African Americans from lower socioeconomic classes, it often is viewed as a substandard dialect. Linguists, however, (Labov, 1972) consider it a dialect different from but not inferior to Standard English. Although the inability to speak Standard English precludes social and vocational access to some situations, the ability to speak two dialects often is an asset. Educators should avoid giving their students the impression that the dialect or language of the home is inferior to the one spoken in school.

As in the case of children who speak a foreign language, children must learn to value their own dialect.

The classroom experience assists them in learning Standard English and what situations are appropriate for use of each dialect (called "code-switching"). Children learn to be "bidialectal" as children from non-English speaking backgrounds learn to be bilingual.

❖ FACILITATING COMMUNICATION IN THE CLASSROOM

This is perhaps the most important discussion in this chapter. How do you, as an early childhood professional, carry out your responsibility of ensuring that children's early communication experiences in the classroom are positive and successful? How do you prepare children from all backgrounds to learn and achieve in the public school setting? How do you assist children learning English as a second language?

You must be well-versed in the kinds of adult-child interactions that facilitate the development of language and communication skills in young children. As the discussion earlier in the chapter suggests, the mainstream middle-class child often comes to the early childhood classroom fully prepared to take advantage of the materials and experiences offered by the program. For this child, you are the coordinator and overseer of meaningful experiences. You arrange the environment that supports and enriches all aspects of development. The healthy mainstream child's own history, expectations, and interaction style are often

nicely in synch with this environment, and his or her understanding of the world and the ability to communicate in it and about it flourishes.

However, your careful arrangement of schedules, materials, and experiences are not sufficient for the child whose early experience or language background does not match that of the classroom. In addition, your interactions with this child, and the ways in which you encourage interactions with other children, are pivotal factors in the child's success. You must be fine-tuned to the needs and preferences, emotions, and messages of this child.

General Strategies that Help All Children Learn Language

Several strategies of adult-child interaction are identified as important in facilitating the kinds of language and communication skills important in the classroom. These are summarized below.

Careful Watching and Listening. The most powerful communicative interactions come from your careful observations of how the child experiences the world and what he or she attempts to communicate. Sensitivity to *nonverbal* cues is particularly important in understanding children from different cultural backgrounds (e.g., Hale, 1982; Cheng, 1987). Although difficult, particularly with large groups of children, *tuning in* and *connecting to* each individual child is critical to development in all areas, especially the area of language. The more you understand how a child experiences the world and what he or she attempts to communicate, the more effective your own communication. Regardless of class size, make it a point to connect with each child several times a day, even if only for a few seconds. This requires careful watching and listening.

Listening *responsively* requires listening for the total meaning of the message. This includes the surface message as it is stated (the meaning of the words) and the undercurrent message (the emotions or feelings associated with the words).

When Wei Ling walks into her classroom on Monday morning, Mrs. Martinez, her teacher, asks her, "How was your weekend, Wei Ling?" Wei Ling responds with an unenthusiastic "Fine." The tone of Wei Ling's response, her facial expression, and her body language suggest that something is troubling her. Noticing the incongruence between her verbal and nonverbal response, Ms. Martinez says, "Do you want to tell me about it?" Wei Ling says "No." Ms. Martinez respects her response but lets her know she cares and is available. She says, "Ok. You can let me know anytime if you want to talk."

Matching Language to Experience. Use words and sentences that match the child's intents, feelings, and experiences by listening carefully to a child's message and watching what he or she is doing. When this match between what is experienced and what is heard occurs, learning takes place more easily. Compare the two examples below:

Nonmatching Sample

Maria: (Trying to scrape mud off her shoes with a stick) "Oh oh."

Teacher: "OK children. It's time to go in and get ready for snack."
(Looking at Maria) "Do you hear me, Maria? Let's go in now."

Matching Sample

Maria: (Trying to scrape mud off her shoes with a stick) "Oh oh."

Teacher: "Oh oh. You got mud on your shoes didn't you. These look like new shoes.

Maria: (Looks at teacher with a worried expression) "Si."

Teacher: "Don't worry, Maria. Let's go inside and someone will help you clean off your shoes. OK?"
(To everyone) "OK children. It's time to go in and get ready for snack."

The additional interaction in the second example took about 15 seconds longer than in the first example. Yet this brief interaction can have significant impact on Maria's language development because she heard words that matched her experience, her feelings, and her communicative intent.

Using Referential Language. Referential language simply means being specific, and using the names of things, as described earlier in this chapter. Although this use of labeling is not necessary to children's learning to talk, it *is* essential to the development of vocabulary and the kinds of language skills necessary for literacy learning in public schools. It takes no more time or effort for the teacher to say, "Put your paints and brushes away now" than to say "Put your things away now."

Use Repetition and Redundancy. Also mentioned earlier in this chapter is the peculiarly middle-class use of repetition and redundancy. Again, although not necessary for children learning to talk, it is a key strategy related to the *enhancement* of language skills. Referring to something more than once and using key words and phrases several times makes language learning much easier. An easy rule for teachers to incorporate is to simply say things more than once, but in slightly different ways. For example:

> "Later today, after recess, we're going to make pudding."
> "OK. We'll make pudding right after recess."

This way, children hear key words more than once and in different sentences.

Another important strategy is "expansion" of children's utterances. A similar strategy is called "progressive matching" (MacDonald, 1985). This involves the use of a more complex phrase or sentence than what the child uses. For example, a child playing outside says "See worm?"

The teacher expands this utterance by saying, "Yes, I see a worm!" If the child says "That's a worm!" the teacher can say "Oh boy! That's a big worm isn't it." This is an effective way of helping children use longer sentence structures because they hear what they just said in a more complex utterance.

Supporting Children from Culturally Different Backgrounds

As discussed earlier in this chapter, many children are unfamiliar with the ways in which language is used in a typical American classroom. Several strategies are helpful in assisting children's successful adjustment to the classroom.

Do Not Pressure Children to Talk. Insisting that young children talk is usually a mistake. It often backfires and makes a child less likely to communicate. It is important, however, that you give children frequent opportunities to talk. Rising intonation patterns and ample pauses encourage children to talk. Perhaps most important, when children are comfortable, having fun, or when there are interesting things to talk about, they are more likely to talk. The following story is a good demonstration of this.

A young Mexican American child enrolled in a Head Start program at the age of four. His mother described him as more shy than her older children, but otherwise a typical child. That did not convince his teacher, however. After six months in the classroom, he had not spoken to an adult, and only infrequently to other children. Carlos' ability to communicate became a major concern for the teacher. She requested consultants to observe him to determine if he needed a referral for testing. One consultant noticed that Carlos seemed unusually sensitive to people watching him. She spoke with Carlos' mother. She said that he spoke at home and did not believe there was a problem. The consultant suggested that the teacher deemphasize efforts to get Carlos to talk and instead, make sure he was fully engaged in activities he enjoyed. One of the teacher assistants discovered that Carlos loved to draw cars and that he was quite good at it. The assistant spent a little time each day, drawing beside Carlos, and using key words that described what they drew. For example, "Four wheels. Four black wheels. And two headlights. I'll make my steering wheel red. You made your steering wheel green? I like the green steering wheel." The assistant did not ask any direct questions, but frequent pauses provided Carlos with the opportunity to talk if he wanted to. No one pressured him to talk. Within a few weeks, Carlos eagerly described his cars and trucks to the assistant.

Avoid Overreliance on Recounts and Eventcasts. It is second nature for teachers to ask children to "Tell us what happened at the zoo" or "Tell us what is happening in this picture?" or "Tell me what you're making." However, as we have pointed out, many children have difficulty using language this way. Teachers must provide many opportunities for children to use language for a wide variety of purposes such as making choices, giving other children directions, entertaining and joking, expressing strong emotions, role playing, and so on.

Allow Children to Use Intermediaries. According to Cheng (1987), Asian children may be reluctant to speak directly to an authority figure and may ask other children to communicate for them. Do not discourage such behavior, but make it explicit that it is okay for the child to approach you directly.

Repeat Favorite Stories Using Props and Actions. Although story-book reading is an important preliteracy activity in the early childhood classroom, include storytelling, as well as story-reading. For younger children and children from different backgrounds, your enthusiastic telling of a story using props (such as objects from the story, puppets, or flannel graph figures) and action (such as acting out key events) is a powerful language teaching tool. The more a story is repeated, the greater its effect. Unfortunately, adults in classrooms become quickly bored with the same stories and songs, and are sometimes reluctant to repeat things as often as children would like. From the child's perspective, however, such repetition has many positive benefits. It creates a sense of security because of its familiarity. It creates a sense of mastery because the child comes to"know" the story perfectly. And it greatly facilitates learning English words and sentences.

Explicitly Model Story Structures. Learning to tell a story with a complex structure and sequence (introduction, setting, sequenced events of plot development, problem resolution, and conclusion) facilitates learning to read and write. Clearly demonstrate the structure of stories for young children not familiar with this format. After children have become familiar with a story, introduce such questions as, "Who are the main characters in this story?" "Where does the story take place?" "What happened first?" and so on.

Create Small Group Problem-solving and Cooperative Learning Projects. Functional communication skills develop best from situations in which there is a real need to communicate. Often, the best such situations are problem-solving ones. Point out a problem such as a leaking faucet or a ball caught in a tree, and ask for ideas for fixing it. Organize older preschool children in groups of two or three to solve such a problem. Or have the children work on a special project. For example, give them the responsibility of deciding what to paint on a mural. The key here is to create meaningful contexts for the use of language.

Avoid Overemphasis of Object Play; Include Social/Affective Themes. While mainstream children like to play with objects such as legos, toy cars and trucks, and materials such as sand, paper, and crayons, many children do not prefer this type of play. For example, according to Hale (1982), some African American like to engage in social interactions that include teasing, turn taking, and verbal volleying. Other children enjoy dramatic play activities with intense emotional themes. For example, a bright, active four-year-old was described as lacking in social skills because during the free play times, he put aside the tasks and materials provided such as puzzles, blocks, bubbles, cars, and trucks. One day the teacher engaged him in some water play using boats and other objects. A toy person fell out of the boat and sank to the bottom of the tank. The teacher exclaimed "Oh no I"m drowning! Help!" Suddenly, this typically disinterested child came to life and talked about saving the drowning man. He played out this theme for some time, expressing a wide range of emotions ranging from fear to anger to happiness as various characters participated in the drama. The teacher introduced key words such as "drowned," "rescue," "sink," and "float." She also had the opportunity to observe a more complex level of play than she had assumed him capable.

Make Maximum Use of Music, "Call and Response," and Choral Responding. In the same way that stories are repeated, sing a few favorite songs every day. Include other songs for variety. Use songs and rhythms that reflect the children's own culture (Hale, 1982). For example, use music with Latin beats, rap music, rock and roll, and Native American drums for dancing; traditional American nursery school songs and rap music for singing and actions, and vocabulary development; and music from East Indian and Asian cultures for quiet times.

Choral responding and chants help children learn sentence frames. African American culture makes use of a "call and response" type of interaction as well as a "verbal volleying" style (Hale, 1982, p.78–79) that is incorporated easily into early childhood programs during circle time and recess activities.

Select Universal Themes and Topics. Children from nonmainstream backgrounds may have difficulty relating to the early childhood classroom because the topics and content of books and projects are not familiar to them. For example, the following common mainstream themes are probably unfamiliar to urban immigrant children: American holidays, vacations, stories about pets, farm animals, and so on. Cheng (1987 p. 142) suggests using story themes that are more universal instead. Such themes include the following:

- eating
- housing
- clothing
- families
- the sun and moon
- rainbows
- weather
- plants and flowers
- colors and numbers
- emotional themes, including fear, sadness, joy, and so on.

Strategies for Helping Young Children Learn English as a Second Language

All the strategies and ideas presented so far in this section are important in assisting the young child learning English as a second language. It is also important to employ staff who speak the child's native language whenever possible. This is important for two reasons. The most obvious, of course, is that a child feels more secure and his needs can be better met if there is a significant adult present who can communicate with him in his own language. The other, perhaps less well-understood, reason is that one of the best ways to ensure success in learning a second language is to develop and maintain a strong foundation in the first language.

Early childhood teachers must recognize the importance of maintaining and valuing the child's language and culture. Garcia (1991) emphasizes that preserving and respecting the child's cultural heritage is crucial to the development of a strong sense of identity. Whenever possible, children's native language development should continue to be supported as they learn English.

Unfortunately in some areas of the United States such as Los Angeles where literally hundreds of different languages are represented, this is not always possible.

Several strategies are particularly helpful for children who speak little English:

Use Strategies Described in This Chapter. It is impossible to overemphasize the point that strategies to facilitate language development for all children are crucial in helping young children learn English as a second language. Read and reread the strategies presented in this chapter.

Respect the Silent Period. Many children learning English as a second language choose not to talk during the early stages of language learning. These children are reflective and cautious. Children with more impulsive, outgoing temperaments, on the other hand, use whatever English words they know, often supplementing with gestures and other nonverbal expressions, as well as words from their native language.

Speak Clearly and Not Too Rapidly. Mumbled speech and rapid rate of speech make it difficult for anyone to understand a foreign language. In the same way, young children whose native language is not English, have a much greater chance of understanding what is said and of eventually learning to speak the language if the teacher speaks clearly and slowly.

Use Comprehensible Input. One of the key points frequently made by Krashen (1981) is the importance of what he calls "comprehensible input". Several simple strategies increase the comprehensibility of language. First, use visual and contextual cues. The context or situation in which the communication is occurring must include multiple nonverbal cues to clarify the meaning of the utterance. For example, the teacher says to a child, "You need to hang your backpack by your cubby." She touches the child's backpack, points to his cubby, and demonstrates by gesturing how to hang it on a hook. Although this example seems obvious, it is amazing how often young, nonnative speakers receive instructions with no nonverbal clue about what is being said.

Also important in this example is the notion of "context-embeddedness". Language is much easier to understand when contained or "embedded" in interesting, meaningful, and immediate contexts. A child can most easily understand language that has something to do with the situation in which he is currently engaged.

Use of short, simple utterances also assist comprehensibility. For example, the sentence above might be simpler to understand if the teacher said, "Please hang your backpack by your cubby." The two sentences "First we will eat lunch. Then we will go outside" are much easier to understand than the more complex sentence, "We will go outside after we eat lunch."

Use Consistent Language to Announce Routine Events. All staff should use similar key words and phrases when referring to common objects and events. For example, hearing "snack," "lunch," and "nutrition" makes it more difficult to learn the term "lunch time." Routine events should be announced in consistent ways. "It's time to go to the bathroom." "Clean up your art materials." "Wash your hands before lunch." If these events are not always announced, or are announced in different ways, a valuable opportunity to assist second language learning is lost.

Another way to use communicative routines to help children learn language is by turning favorite stories or field trips into "play scripts." A common pretend play theme is playing grocery store. Using a play script involves children learning certain "lines," as if they were in a play. For example, "Could you please help me find the cereal?" "That will be three dollars and fifty cents, please." "Thank you. Have a nice day." Another example is acting out the story of *Goldilocks and the Three Bears*. While fluent speakers ad lib and vary the lines of the script, repeating them frequently assists the second language learner.

The frequent use of carefully selected nursery rhymes is also helpful to the child learning English as a second language. They are fun when done as a group recitation. In addition, the repetition and simple language provides important opportunities for nonnative speakers to learn English sentence frames.

Compare Native and English Language Vocabulary. Help all children develop a "metalinguistic" awareness, even at the preschool level. Metalinguistic awareness is a conscious awareness of words and sentences as language. One simple way to facilitate this awareness is by demonstrating different words for things. For example, show the class a shoe and say, "In English we say 'shoe' and in Spanish we say 'zapato.'"

Avoid Correcting Children's Grammar. Correcting a child's grammar or asking him to say something "the right way" is not likely to facilitate second language acquisition in young children. In many cases, it actually interferes with language learning. A more effective strategy is to model the correct form.

Teacher:	"Are you going to your grandmother's this weekend?"
Child:	"I go she house."
Teacher:	"You're going to her house? You like going to her house don't you."
Child:	"Yes. I like going her house!"

In this way, the child hears the corrected form, but communication is not interrupted or discouraged.

❖ CHAPTER SUMMARY

The development of communication skills is critical to children's school achievement and social success. Communication skills relate not only to the particular language spoken or the stage of language development, but also to the ways in which and purposes for which language is used. Language is a set of complex skills influenced in many ways by culture and family interactions. The early experiences of young mainstream children often adapt to preschool expectations for language use and performance. However, there often is a mismatch between nonmainstream children's skills and early experiences, and the expectations of the preschool. In addition, the nature of the mismatch varies from culture to culture and child to child. Early childhood teachers should examine and understand fully their own expectations and assumptions regarding how children use language. Equally important, teachers should utilize a variety of strategies to maximize the potential for each child's comfort and achievement in the classroom, as well as nurture the continued communication skills development of *all* children.

❖ REFERENCES

Au, K. H., & Jordan, C. (1981). Teaching reading to Hawaiian children: Finding culturally appropriate solutions In H. T. Trueba, G. P. Guthrie, & K. H. Au (eds.), *Culture and the bilingual classroom: Studies in classroom ethnography* (pp. 139–152). Boston: Newbury House.

Brown, R. (1973). *A first language: The early stages.* Cambridge, MA: Harvard University Press.

Cheng, L. R. (1987). *Assessing Asian language performance.* Rockville MD: Aspen Publishers.

Cheng, L. (1997). Diversity: Challenges and implications for assessment. *Journal of Children's Communicative Development, 19*(1), 55–62.

Crago, M. (1992). Ethnography and language socialization: A cross-cultural perspective. *Topics in Language Disorders, 12,* 28–39.

Cross, T. (1984). Habilitating the language impaired child: Ideas from studies of parent-child interaction. *Topics in Language Disorders, 4,* 1–14.

Cummins, J. (1984). *Bilingualism and special education: Issues in assessment and pedagogy.* Clevedon Avon, England: Multilingual Matters.

Dellacorte, M., Benedict, H., & Klein, M. D., (1983). The relationship of pragmatic dimensions of mothers' speech to the referential-expressive distinction. *Journal of Child Language, 10,* 35–43.

Eisenberg, A. (1982). Language development in cultural perspective: Talk in three Mexicano Homes. Unpublished Ph.D. Dissertation. Berkeley: University of California.

Garcia, E. E. (1991). Caring for infants in a bilingual child-care setting. *The Journal of Educational Issues of Language Minority Students, 9,* 1–10

Genesee, F., & Nicoladis, E. (1995). Language development in bilingual preschool children. In E. Garcia & B. McLaughlin (eds.), *Meeting the challenge of linguistic and cultural diversity in early childhood education.* New York: Teachers College Press.

Gottfried, A. W. (Ed.). (1984). *Home environment and early cognitive research.* Orlando, FL: Academic Press.

Gutierrez-Clellen, V. F., & Quinn, R. (1993) Assessing narratives of children from diverse cultural/linguistic groups. *Language Speech, and Hearing Services in Schools, 24,* 2–9.

Hakuta, K., & Garcia, E. (1989). Bilingualism and education. *American Psychologist, 44*(2), 374–79.

Hale, J. (1982). *Black children: Their roots, culture and learning style.* Provo, UT: Brigham Young University Press.

Haynes, W., & Saunders, D. (1999). Joint book-reading strategies in middle-class African American and White mother-toddler dyads. *Journal of Children's Communication Development, 20*(2), 9–18.

Heath, S. B. (1983). *Ways with Words: Language, life and work in communities and classrooms.* Cambridge, UK: Cambridge University Press.

Heath, S. B. (1986). Sociocultural contexts of language development. In California State Department Bilingual Education Office (ed.), *Beyond language: Social and cultural factors in schooling language minority students* (pp. 143–186). Los Angeles: Evaluation, Dissemination and Assessment Center, California State University, Los Angeles.

Iglesias, A. (1985a). Cultural conflict in the classroom: The communicatively different child. In D. Ripich & F. Spinelli (eds.), *School discourse problems* (pp. 79–96). San Diego: College Hill.

Iglesias, A. (1985b). Communication in the home and classroom: Match or Mismatch? *Topics in Language Disorders, 5*(4), 29–41.

Krashen, S. (1981). Bilingual education and second language acquisition theory. In California State Department of Education Office of Bilingual Bicultural Education (ed.), *Schooling and language minority students: A theoretical framework.* Los Angeles: Evaluation, Dissemination and Assessment Center, California State University.

Krashen, S. (1992). *Fundamentals of language education.* Torrance, CA: Laredo Publishing.

Labov, W. (1972). The logic of nonstandard English. In P. P. Giglioli (ed.), *Language and social context* (pp. 179–215). Baltimore: Penguin Books.

Lein, L. (1978). Children's disputes in three speech communities. *Language in Society 9*(3) 299–323.

Lemlech, J. (1977). *Handbook for successful urban teaching.* New York: Harper and Row

MacDonald, J. A. (1985). Language through conversation. A model for intervention with language-delayed persons. In S. F. Warren & A. K. Rogers-Warren (eds.), *Teaching functional language* (pp. 89–122). Baltimore: University Park Press.

Mehan, H. (1979). *Learning lessons: Social organization in the classroom.* Cambridge, MA: Harvard University Press.

NAEYC. (1996). NAEYC Position Statement: Responding to linguistic and cultural diversity-recommendations for effective early childhood education. *Young Children, 51*(4), 4–12.

Ochs, E. (1982). Talking to children in Western Samoa. *Language in Society,* 11, 77–104.

Pena, E. D., & Quinn, R. (1997). Task familiarity: Effects on the test performance of Puerto Rican and African American children. *Language, Speech and Hearing Services in School,* 28, 323–332

Peregoy, S. F., & Boyle, O. F. (1993). *Reading, writing and learning in ESL.* New York: Academic Press.

Saracho, O., & Hancock, F. M. (1983). Mexican American culture. In O. Saracho & B. Spodek (eds), *Understanding the multicultural experience in early childhood education* (pp. 3–16). Washington DC: National Association for the Education of Young Children.

Schieffelin, B. B. (1990). *The give and take of everyday life: Language socialization of Kaluli children.* Cambridge: Cambridge University Press.

Tabors, P. O. (1977). *One child, two languages. A guide for preschool educators of children learning English as a second language.* Baltimore: Paul H. Brookes Publishing.

Tafoya, T. (1983). Coyote in the classroom: The use of Native American oral tradition with young children. In O. N. Saracho & B. Spodek (eds.), *Understanding the multicultural experience in early childhood education* (pp. 35–44). Washington DC: National Association for Education of Young Children.

Tattershall, S., and Creaghead, N. (1985). A comparison of communication at home and school. In D. Ripich & F. Spinelli (eds.), *School discourse problems.* San Diego: College Hill.

Westby, C. (1985). Cultural differences in caregiver-child interaction: Implications for assessment and intervention. Paper presented at the annual convention of the American Speech-Language-Hearing Association. Albuquerque, NM.

Chapter **6**

School Readiness and Emergent Literacy

One of the points at which diversity is most apparent is when children enter formal schooling. As children begin kindergarten, they bring with them five years of experience. For some children, that experience is matched to the expectations of the school classroom. For others it is not. As is stressed throughout this text, the issue of mismatch between children's early experience and school expectations seriously threaten the potential for school achievement. The area of literacy readiness is particularly vulnerable to children's early experiences. In addition, children's social adjustment to formal schooling is dependent on early experience. Neuman and Roskos (1994) suggest the need "to ease the fundamental discontinuity between home and school learning contexts with a culturally responsive approach" (p.210). Such an approach includes the following features:

1. It respects children's home culture by building on the uses of language and literacy with which they are already familiar. Neuman and Roskos (1994) give an example of using African American street games with a distinctive type of rhyme as the basis for learning about the sounds in words.

2. It engages children in language and literacy activities that foster collaboration and sharing of cultural perspectives. In this way, differences are acknowledged and valued. Learning new ways of doing things and viewing the world is a desirable outcome that enhances all participants. Therefore, diversity is not simply accepted and tolerated; it is sought after and preferred.

3. The goals of literacy and academic achievement are the same for all children. A culturally responsive approach does not imply lower standards for children from nonmainstream backgrounds. Instead, it sets the same standards of achievement for all participants, even though the means of achieving them may be different.

Phillips (1994) discussed the importance of African American children becoming bicultural; that is, being able to switch language and behavioral styles in ways that empower them to be successful in both their home and school cultures. Therefore, the goal of the early educator is not just to "bridge the gap" between home and school. The notion of bridging the gap implies that the home culture must be compensated for, and that the child must gradually be transformed in ways that better fit school expectations. However, the belief of many in the field of multicultural education is that the goal of early education is to value and maintain the child's home culture, while gradually providing students with knowledge and skills which enable children to adapt, when necessary, to the demands of mainstream institutions. In the longer term, an ideal which might be sought after by schools and other institutions is the recognition of the benefit of incorporating diverse values into their own value systems (Boykin, 1994).

Families from all backgrounds value education and desire that their children do well (Reese, Balzano, Gallimore, & Goldenberg, 1991). However, the ways in which families prepare children to participate in formal schooling vary significantly (e.g., Snow, Barnes, Chandler, Goodman, & Hemphill, 1991; Teale, 1986). Reese, et al. (1991) studied 121 Latino immigrant families. This careful ethnographic study of the family values and activities related to schooling challenges the commonly held notion that traditional agrarian values such as filial piety and family unity, emphasis on learning manners, and respectful behavior and cooperation are incompatible with the competitive, individualistic, achievement-oriented values associated with academic success in American schools. Reese, et al. (1991) conclude that in homes where children are doing well, families have been able to incorporate certain mainstream values related to school achievement while at the same time drawing strength from such traditional values as extended family ties and family unity and respect. Snow, et al. describe two low-income families with similar challenging circumstances. One family provides their children with ample support for literacy development; the other does not. Therefore, it is clear that nonmainstream status, or even poverty, need not be associated with poor school success.

This chapter considers ways in which early childhood professionals can support the successful adjustment of young children from diverse backgrounds to formal schooling. Particular attention is in the area of literacy readiness.

❖ EMERGENT LITERACY

Morrison (1991) suggested that literacy is the "hot topic" among early educators (p.91). This is partly in response to the fast growing numbers of children who enter school without the kinds of communication skills and early experiences that prepare them to succeed in formal literacy education.

A term that reflects the increasing emphasis on the relationship of early experience to literacy is "emergent literacy" (Clay, 1979, 1989; Sulzby, 1985; van Kleeck, 1990). Literacy is not simply an accumulation of the specific skills related to encoding and decoding print. It evolves through the sociocultural and cognitive processes that begin at birth. Literacy evolves gradually as a function of exposure to, and interaction with, print materials and exposure to other children and adults who are using print; that is, "literacy events." This gradual emergence of literacy skills is observed early in development as young children recognize pictures, look at books, recognize logos (for example, McDonalds' Golden Arches), draw and scribble, and so on.

Most children from middle-class mainstream homes come to school with these emergent literacy skills well-established. They have an awareness of print and its importance, and have developed an interest in learning the mechanics of reading and writing.They have already begun the process of learning sound-letter association, letter recognition, and how to write their names. Indeed, they are ready to begin where their teachers are prepared to teach. Children from many nonmainstream homes, however, often have not developed the same kinds of skills and are unfamiliar with middle-class literacy materials (Snow, 1993). (See Adams, 1990, and the 1998 report of the National Research Council for extensive discussion of the early experiences and skills associated with literacy development.) Elementary school teachers are seldom equipped to provide the experiences necessary to bridge the resulting gap. Children are far behind before they even begin, and "catching up" is difficult (Rush, 1999). The gap often widens rather than narrows as children move through the grades.

In addition to these emergent literacy skills, an important foundation for the development of literacy is laid through the development of what is called "literate style oral language" (Cook-Gumperz, Gumperz, & Simons, 1981), also referred to as "autonomous" or "decontextualized" language. This is the language used in formal schooling. Informal language in the home is characterized more by an "interpersonal" style in which there are many shared meanings among speakers. Such language does not rely on words alone, but on gestures, facial expressions, and so on. The meaning is understood by the listeners without unnecessary words. On the other hand, the language of formal schooling that supports the transition to literacy comprises complete sentences, accurate descriptive vocabulary, and expresses the sequences and relationships among ideas in narrative.

In this chapter, we focus primarily on how early experience prepares young children for the development of literacy skills, and how you, as an early childhood professional, can bridge the gap that often exists between children's emergent literacy skills and classroom expectations in kindergarten and first grade. This occurs by affirming and building on the child's home culture and experience. First, let us review several points related to children's use of language.

Cultural Variations in Children's Use of Language

In an earlier chapter, we discussed the kinds of communication skills valued by mainstream society and considered important for developmental achievements in preparation for school success. These include the following:

- verbal assertiveness or the ability to carry on conversations with adults
- use of labels and precise vocabulary
- "autonomous" language skills or the ability to use language with such accuracy and precision that it "stands alone" without props, gestures, or shared experience with the listener
- narrative skills or the ability to tell stories or give explanations in ways that are clear to the listener and reflect conventional structure of beginning, middle, and end and the use of "cohesive devices" such as "because," "and so," "if," and

"then" to express specific relationships among ideas (Cook-Gumperz, Gumperz, & Gumperz, 1981). Often, children provide narrative "recounts" of an event with which the adult listener is already familiar (Heath 1986a)

- the ability to "talk about the obvious" or to describe something the adult experiences at the same time such as the child describing what he or she is draws. Heath (1986) refers to this as an "eventcast."

Many of these ways of using language may be uncommon in some families. For example:

- initiating conversations with adults may be considered inappropriate;
- talking about the obvious may be considered insulting or bizarre;
- the primary means of conveying information may be nonverbal (for example, modeling and demonstrating instead of talking);
- story structures may be circular or episodic instead of linear (sequential) or hierarchical (Boykin, 1994);
- communication through storytelling depends on shared experience, props and materials, body movements, and audience participation; and
- "good" communication is that in which meaning is implicit rather than detailed and explicit.

The characteristics of language expected at the time of school entry form an important part of the very foundation for the ways in which we teach reading and writing in United States schools. Yet they are uncommon in the home environments of many children and the relative disadvantage grows ever wider. Language differences interfere with successful classroom communication and social interactions and they jeopardize a child's successful transition into literacy.

There is a body of research suggesting that certain kinds of early communicative experiences are related to successful reading achievement in school. One important longitudinal study was reported by Snow, et al. (1991). This study examined home factors related to elementary school reading achievement and concluded that one of the strongest factors related to fostering literacy was conversations between adults and children about the content of books and shared experiences. Snow (1983) suggested earlier that the same processes that support early language development ("semantic contingency" or responsiveness to topic introduced by the child), scaffolding, and use of language in predictable routines, also support the development of literacy. Snow & Ninio (1986) concluded that the child's development of "autonomous" language skills are particularly important: "The ability to understand and produce decontextualized language may be the most difficult and most crucial prerequisite to literacy" (p. 119).

Strategies Supporting the Development of Language Skills Related to Literacy Development

Early childhood professionals can do much to support the development of what is called "literate style oral language." It is important to begin by utilizing language forms and communication activities already familiar to the child. For example, in the important area of narrative skills, determine what kinds of narrative forms are used in the child's home. If there is a favorite family tale, or if an interesting event has occurred, use this as the basis for practicing narratives. The challenge is to identify ways of communicating familiar to the child; to respect and incorporate those various styles into the classroom; and bridge the gap by assisting the child to learn expected school language genres in ways that expand rather than replace his or her existing communicative repertoires.

Use of Decontextualized "Autonomous" Language. Teachers can incorporate games and activities into the classroom that require the use of precise, decontextualized speech. For example:

1. Modify games like Simon Says to require more descriptive language.
2. Play a referential language game that requires one child to explain to others how to build a block construction to look just like his. Put his construction behind a screen so the other children cannot see it. Ask him to give clear enough instructions so the other children can reproduce it

correctly; for example, "Put a red square block first. Then put a long blue one on top." This provides a challenging way of using language without other cues.

3. For younger play children, talking on a *toy* telephone to introduce decontextualized language. For older children, talk on a *real* telephone to the teacher or classroom assistant to teach children to use words alone to convey a message.

4. Create the need for children to make requests that require some description. For example, before lunch, show the children there are two kinds of cookies available for dessert: "cookies with chocolate chips" and "cookies with raisins." After each child finishes lunch, ask, "What do you want for dessert?" Remind him of the choices, but keep the cookies out of sight, thereby requiring precise use of language in a motivating situation.

5. For more verbal children, ask them to take a message to another adult. For example, "Please go ask Miss Perez if we can borrow her scissors." If necessary, model the actual words the child might use; for example, "Say to Miss Perez, 'May we borrow your scissors?'"

Narratives.

1. Ask parents if there are favorite family stories or significant recent events in the children's lives.

—Encourage each child to tell about an event in whatever style is most natural. Practice the story over time.

—Be flexible about the social context. If the child is not comfortable telling the story to a group, encourage him or her to tell it to his favorite adult or peer. Or have children act out the story in a small group.

—Help the child incorporate various props and actions as he or she "perfects" his story. For example, draw pictures or cut out pictures from a magazine, or develop actions and sounds that go along with the key events of the story. Some parts of a story may not need words, only silence and movement.

—Include rhyme or rhythm in the story if this appeals to the child.

—Once the teacher and other children learn the child's story, include it in the classroom repertoire.

2. Select certain stories that clearly reflect the linear sequence of beginning, middle, and end, and read them to the class.

—Use "metalinguistic" strategies to talk about the story structure. For example, explain that many stories have a beginning (where the story starts), a middle part (where something important happens), and an ending (where a problem is solved or a certain result occurs and the story is over). Model the narrative structures (e.g., how to do "show and tell") you want to encourage in the children. (Heath, 1986).

—Use key phrases like "Once upon a time," "And then . . .," and "That's the end" to exaggerate and provide clear markers for the elements of the story structure.

—Read these stories frequently, using a flannel board to place pictures of key elements in the story sequence.

—As children become more familiar with the story, encourage them to anticipate "What happens next?" They can respond with key words, sounds and noises, or take turns placing pictures on the board at the right moment.

—As stories become more familiar, have the children take turns being "teacher" and telling the story themselves.

3. Watch short captivating videos or parts of favorite videos children bring from home.

—Help children discuss the interesting elements of the video.

—Review the video using a brief story structure that sequences the key elements.

4. Use repetition and elaboration of favorite pretend play scenarios to create play scripts that reflect typical story structures such as going to the grocery store, having a tea party, and so on.

Supporting Phoneme Awareness

Speech sound awareness is another area in which there is wide variance among children. Chaney (1990) suggests that despite greater emphasis on emergent literacy and whole language approaches to reading instruction, children will still need assistance in the area of phonological awareness and sound-letter association.

If a phonics approach is taken to early reading instruction in the K-1 classroom, the child who cannot perceive and segment individual speech sounds, or "phonemes" (that is, to perceive that the word "dog" is made up of three sounds: "d" + "aw" + "g"), is at a significant disadvantage. Phoneme awareness is not automatic. The normal unit of speech perception is the syllable, not the phoneme. For example, as we listen to the word "mama," our perception is of two repetitions of the syllable "ma;" it is not of the sound sequence "m"-"ah"- "m"-"ah.". A child must *learn* to segment syllables into individual phonemes. This ability is an absolute prerequisite to learning the skill of sound-letter association required by a phonics approach to reading (the letter "M" makes the "mmmm" sound, and so on). Unfortunately, this is a very difficult task for many young children.

The following are fun ways of helping young children become more aware of these sound segments prior to eventual formal reading instruction.

1. Begin with recognition of environmental sounds. Ask children to close their eyes. Select one of several noise-making items (hit a triangle, ring a bell,

shake a box of cereal, or beat a drum). Ask the children to guess which item made that sound. Lead a discussion about how sounds are similar and how they are different.

2. Include rhymes in daily circle time. Help children become aware of rhyming words. Watson et al. (1994) suggest making ample use of Dr. Seuss books, nursery rhymes and poetry, and chants.

   —Whenever possible, use material from the children's own culture. Ask parents for suggestions, and explain the importance of directing children's attention to the way words sound.

   —Ask children to think of words or nonsense syllables that rhyme with a certain word ("Who can think of a word that rhymes with 'dog?'").

   —Point out rhymes that occur throughout the day. For example, say to one child, "Gail, can you bring me the pail." Show pleasure that you made a rhyme. Directing children's attention in this way develops speech sound awareness and fosters an enjoyment of listening to and analyzing the sounds in words.

3. Play imitation games which require groups of children to listen carefully and reproduce sound patterns of nonsense syllables that gradually increase in difficulty. For example, begin with "Fee Fi Fo Fum." Then try "Fee Fo Fi Fum," then "Gee Gi Bo Hum," and so on. This strategy provides a playful way for children to practice sounds difficult for them to produce such as an English phoneme that does not occur in their native language.

❖ CULTURAL INFLUENCES ON EMERGENT LITERACY

As discussed earlier, in addition to language skills, emergent literacy skills are of critical importance to children's preparation for formal literacy instruction in school. According to Morrison (1991), literacy development is a natural social and cognitive process that begins at birth. These skills emerge as a function of children's exposure to and interaction with other people engaged in literacy activities. It should be noted it is not the mere exposure to literacy materials and activities, but the social interaction that occurs around these events (van Kleek, 1990).

Development of Emergent Literacy Skills

Although the sequence and ages of emergent literacy skills related to reading and writing are not the same for all children, several researchers describe common early skills often demonstrated by young children (for example, Clay, 1989). Cook, Tessier, and Klein (2000) provide an example of one child's sequence of emergent literacy development in Figure 6-1 (see also Notari-Syverson, O'Connor, and Vadasy, 1998, for a preschool literacy checklist).

SAMPLE OF EMERGENT LITERACY
Sequence of Emergence of Reading and
Writing for One Child

Reading
1. Enjoys looking at books
2. Listens carefully to story and looks at pictures
3. Holds book right side up; turns pages from front to back
4. Talks about pictures
5. Retells favorite stories by looking at pictures
6. Recognizes environmental print (McDonalds and Coke)
7. Tries to rhyme words
8. Pretends to "read" story books
9. Recognizes key words in familiar book
10. Associates "ss" and "puh" sound to initial letters S and P

Writing
1. Scribbles with magic marker
2. Makes lines and circles
3. Draws a face
4. Adds arms and legs to face
5. Draws a house
6. Pretends to write letters to friends using wavy lines
7. Practices making letter-like forms
8. Includes some real letters
9. Writes own name and the word "MOM"

The sequence of skills listed above reflects the basic elements of emergent literacy development as follows:

Reading

1. Appreciation and understanding of picture representation of objects and events.
2. Understanding of, and ability to use, narrative to represent sequence of events.
3. Interest in books and book skills; for example, identifies beginning of book, turns pages from left to right, turns pages one at a time, and so on.
4. Recognizes "environmental print" such as abstract logos and symbols for things such as stop signs, men's/women's restroom, foods (coke), restaurants and stores (K-Mart, McDonalds), products (Nike tennis shoes, Playdough), television shows (cartoons, Sesame Street title, Barney), open/closed sign in store window, and exit sign.
5. Becomes interested in print in books; begins to understand there is some relationship between print and pictures in storybook.
6. Recognizes own name in print.
7. Recognizes key words in storybook print.
8. Begins to match and recognize certain letters; asks adult for letter names.
9. Begins to make sound-letter associations for initial letters of words (knows "P" at beginning of word makes "puh" sound).

Writing

1. Plays with writing utensils and tries to mark on paper and other surfaces with crayons, markers, paint brush, and the like.
2. Gradually gains more fine motor control; makes lines and circles.
3. Draws a face; later adds arms and legs.
4. Draws house, flowers, and so on.
5. Tells a story about the drawing.
6. Engages in "pretend writing" (pretends to write a letter) by making wavy lines.
7. Scribbles look more like letters; adds letters to drawings.
8. Writes own name; practices writing certain letters.

It is clear that the kinds of skills and understanding described above are very much dependent on children's early experiences and opportunities to develop such skills.

The Role of Early Experience and the Development of Literacy

In recent years, research shows that the roots of emergent literacy skills lie in the social interactions that occur in families around literacy events. Many studies examined the relationship between early experience and the development of literacy skills. The positive relationship between parent-child communication around literacy events in the home and later development of reading and writing is quite clear. Research by Wells (1982, 1985) and Mason (1992) demonstrate that literacy related activities, particularly storybook reading, supports the development of reflective think-

ing necessary for school success. Snow and Ninio (1986) conclude that early parent-child interactions around literacy events support the development of decontextualized language skills. In a longitudinal study of elementary school children, Snow, et al. (1991) reported that the opportunity to interact with adults, parent provision of literacy events, and materials for children and maternal expectations were related to students' reading achievement.

A study reported by Hildebrandt and Bader (1992) found that preschool children whose parents read to them, took them to the library, provided alphabet books, and discussed television shows were more likely to demonstrate early literacy skills such as writing their names, writing letters, and asking for help in reading signs. A study reported by Williams (1991) described the processes by which middle-class black mothers establish children's identity as a "literate person."

It is clear that children's early home environment, and particularly parent child interactions, relate to their development of literacy. It is also clear there is great variation in the ways in which, and the extent to which, families engage in the kinds of activities that support later achievement in literacy.

Especially in low-income homes, many families do not read to their children or model reading for pleasure. For example, Teale (1986) reported that in a study of 24 low-income families from various cultural backgrounds, children were read to on any regular basis in only three of the families. Interestingly, anecdotal descriptions of the three children from these families suggested their emergent literacy skills were superior to other children in the study. Dickinson, DeTemple, Hirschler, and Smith (1992) found that when the low-income caregivers in the study read to their children, language was restricted to questions asking the child for recall of specific details or labels instead of elaborating on the elements of the story or predicting outcomes. Also, many caregivers were unable to increase the cognitive demands of their discussions as the children got older.

A study reported by Anderson and Stokes (1984) found ethnic differences in the frequency of literacy events, with Anglo families engaging in twice as many literacy events as Hispanic or African American families.

Cultural Influences on Early Literacy Experiences

Anderson and Stokes (1984) examined the occurrence of literacy events in families from different cultural and ethnic backgrounds. The results of this study revealed a variety of sources of literacy. These are summarized below:

1. *Daily living activities* such as making lists for grocery shopping; reading labels and recipes; going to various public services offices such as the departments of welfare, employment, and motor vehicles; and paying bills.
2. *Entertainment* such as reading newspaper movie listings; television guides and books; doing crossword puzzles; and reading subtitles or credits on films or videos.
3. *Religious activities* such as attending Bible study groups, singing hymns, and reading daily devotions books.
4. *Work-related activities* such a writing checks, reading instructions, following delivery instructions, and stocking shelves.
5. *School-related activities* such as doing homework or playing "school."
6. *Interpersonal communications* such as writing and reading notes, letters, and birthday cards.
7. *Storybook time* in which parents read to children, primarily for their entertainment.
8. *Literacy techniques and skills* including activities in which reading or writing is the specific focus of the interaction. Such activities often are initiated by the child ("What is this word?' or "How do you make a "T?").

The findings of this descriptive study are important because they provide insight into potential sources of emergent literacy skills other than traditional book-reading.

While it is well established that there is a relationship between storybook reading in the home and literacy development in children, it is also clear that this may not be a common activity in many families. Teale (1986) points out the ways in which poverty can limit children's access to literacy events. For example, money provides more leisure time, more opportunity for travel, more frequent eating out and exposure to menus, and so forth. White-collar jobs require parents to read more when compared to blue-collar work, and so on. However, Teale also notes that low-income homes *can be* homes of high literacy. The challenge for early childhood professionals, then, is to find ways of building on the literacy activities that occur in children's homes such as those described earlier by Anderson and Stokes (1984). Preschool classroom activities can provide print-rich environments to help children make the transition from home to formal schooling.

Intervention Strategies

Intervention strategies must be designed to bridge the gap between children's early experiences and school expectations in ways that *affirm and expand home culture and experience.* The following are some suggestions (in addition to earlier suggestions in this chapter related to supporting language development):

1. First, determine how children currently experience literacy in their homes. Observations during home visits or conversations with parents and with children reveal which of the possible sources of literacy described by Anderson and Stokes above are familiar activities for each child (for example, recipes, grocery lists, newspapers, *TV Guide*, letterwriting, and so on). Incorporate those activities and materials into the classroom and find interesting ways to expand on them.

2. Select stories and storybooks that are interesting and relevant to children's lives at home. In some instances, let children compose their own stories. A fun activity is to look for pictures in magazines or draw pictures that depict the story elements. Once the pictures are produced and pasted on large sheets of paper, write key words and phrases (thereby producing customized "big books") to read in circle time, small groups, or with individual children.

3. Provide parents with copies of small, easy-to-read books used in the classroom. Translate the books into the child's home language. An intervention study reported by McCormick and Mason (1986) reported that low-income prekindergarten children, whose parents were given "little books" prior to kindergarten entry, did much better in first grade than a control group. In this study, the books were made by the researchers and included very simple pictures and minimal print.

   —In another intervention study reported by Dickinson, et al. (1992), a home-school partnership model was designed for low-income families. In this model, mothers received books for their children. Teachers then followed up and reinforced concepts in those same books. The following is an example of text from one of the books used in the McCormick and Mason (1986, p. 115) study:

   "TIME FOR BED
   Brush your teeth
   Read a story
   Get a hug
   Climb in bed
   Nighty-night, sleep tight!"

—At this simple level, text is created to reflect concepts and events meaningful to the child and which reflect the home environment.

4. Another strategy reflects the importance of demonstrating to children the *utility* of reading and writing. This involves the teacher modeling the various functions of print in her own life and demonstrating how print is relevant and valuable to children. For example, adults in the classroom can model the functions of print by:

—reading notes from parents and staff;

—looking in the newspaper for coupons;

—writing a note to oneself as a reminder; then discovering the note later in the day;

—discovering what is served for lunch;

—reading the funnies in the newspaper; and

—ordering items from a catalogue.

Teachers can easily involve children in these literacy activities in enjoyable ways. In addition, they must devise ways of demonstrating the value of literacy to the children themselves. The following are examples:

—Help children read material they bring from home such as a letter from grandma, a daily prayer book, the *TV Guide*, and so on.

—Read clues for a treasure hunt. This is a highly motivating demonstration of the function of literacy because the reward can only by discovered by reading the written clues.

—Invite children to find their own name card at the beginning of circle time and post it to mark attendance. Identify other children's name cards to determine who is absent.

—Identify name cards to see who gets to do the special duties each day.

—Ask children to request favorite songs or stories by selecting cards that display the title with a small drawing in the corner of the card.

—Play post office and mailman during pretend play in which children pretend to write letters, mail them, deliver them, and read them.

—Include a variety of books in the house corner in addition to children's story books such as cookbooks, phone books, *TV Guide*, catalogues, magazines, and so on. Whenever possible,

books should be in the children's home language and reflect the home community.

—Create a writing center that includes stationary, envelopes, pens, and pretend stamps. Allow children to dictate letters to their family members or to pretend to write them themselves.

—Help children write real letters and actually mail them to themselves (or to a family member). Alert the caregiver at home to watch for the letter in the mail.

—Make shopping lists with children, then go on a field trip to look for those items. For example, make a grocery list of ingredients for a favorite recipe. Go to the store, buy the items, return, and follow the recipe to make the dish.

—Help children recognize grocery store items by pointing out logos on packaging.

—Ask parents to provide empty packages of food they use at home so that the pretend store in the classroom has some items reflecting each child's community.

—Make picture books out of photographs. Children can bring photos from home or teachers can take Polaroid pictures of important people and events in the children's lives. Make these into sequenced picture books. Write key words and phrases on the pages and ask children to "read" the story themselves.

—Translate books with repeated phrases into the child's native language.

—Read favorite books over and over. Include discussion of pictures and vocabulary. Elaborate on ideas in the book. Relate the book to the children's own lives. Ask questions like, "Does this make you think of anything at your house?" "Is this_____ like yours, or is it different?"

—Use "metalinguistic" strategies to talk explicitly about the "concepts of print:" "This first page is the beginning of the book." "Let's turn to the next page." "This page has lots of words on it." "Who can guess what the words on this page say?" "This is the last page so it's the end of the story."

The list of meaningful ways to support children's development of emergent literacy skills is endless. Look up the excellent article by Watson, Layton, Pierce, and Linzy (1994) that provides additional ideas for incorporating literacy activities in each component of the preschool program.

❖ SOCIAL ASPECTS OF SCHOOL READINESS

Chapter 4 examined various cultural influences on young children's social skills. As the young child enters kindergarten and begins formal schooling, certain social skills, particularly those related to teacher-student interaction, relate to children's early school success.

Teacher-student interaction in a typical American classroom relies on a test question format (Mehan 1979) in which individual students are asked to recite verbally (for example, "Joanne, what is two plus two?" Or "What is the next word?"). This format is particularly uncomfortable for many children. Au and Kawakami (1994) and Pewewardy (1994) point out that many Native American children are uncomfortable being singled out in front of their peers. Instead, allow students to collaborate in producing answers to your questions.

Carrasco, Vera, and Cazden (1981) found that students from Latino backgrounds were more comfortable in classrooms in which teachers' interactions expressed concern for their well-being and their families. Au and Kawakami (1994) point out that many children are more comfortable interacting with peers or older siblings than with adults. In light of this, it is important to take advantage of peer group dynamics as much as possible in the classroom.

Shade (1994) and others have stressed the importance of using high levels of physical activity to stimulate the interest of African American students. Another important difference often noted in children from nonmainstream backgrounds is a greater response to nonverbal communication than to the traditional use of exclusively oral communication. Therefore, when giving instructions, it is important to *show* children what is expected of them instead of simply telling them. Barrera (1993) suggests that some children need to observe other children for a period of time before they try something themselves.

❖ LINKING HOME AND SCHOOL TO SUPPORT CHILDREN'S SOCIAL IDENTITY

Early childhood professionals should be aware of the difficulties young children from diverse cultural backgrounds face as they begin formal schooling. They can do much to make children's first experiences with the classroom positive ones by using the kinds of strategies that take their home experiences, history, and individual learning styles into consideration. In addition, early childhood professionals can gradually acculturate children to the kinds of interactions and behavioral demands experienced in the kindergarten classroom. Barrera (1993) stresses the importance of realizing that, as young children begin school, they often experience significant stress when behaviors associated with competence in one environment are unacceptable in a different environment. Young children in the process of developing their individual and social identities experience stress and confusion if they feel the experience and behaviors they bring from home are unacceptable in the classroom.

Neuman and Roskos (1994) make several suggestions for classroom strategies that help children affirm their own culture while learning to understand and function in the mainstream:

1. Develop a "Me-museum," an area of the classroom that highlights one or two children each week. Ask parents to contribute items important to the featured child. This includes photos of family members, favorite toys, music, and foods. Invite family members to come to class and talk about the child and the family. In this way, every child is valued for his or her uniqueness and learns more about each other and the range of diversity represented in the class.

2. Include a variety of multiethnic literature in children storybooks. Include discussions of how children in the class are similar or different from characters in the book such as how they look, how they feel, and how they behave in similar circumstances. In this way, literature and the process of reading always connects to the children's own lives.

3. Create "big" books related to themes. Have each child contribute his or her own page. Themes could include favorite foods, favorite sayings, drawings of children's "dream house," self-portraits, and so on.

4. Involve parents in literacy activities by helping children make a "family album." Have parents help children find photos, memorabilia, and magazine pictures to represent home and community. Paste these on construction paper and place in plastic zip-lock bags to become the pages of the album. Have family members write captions on the pages. Another idea is "prop boxes." Ask families to provide items related to a particular theme, such as the child's birthday or favorite holiday. The items in the box become the source of language written down by the teacher.

❖ PARENT INVOLVEMENT IN SCHOOLING

The importance of family involvement in children's schooling cannot be overstated. Early childhood professionals must provide information and strategies to nonmainstream parents regarding ways of interacting with their children that help close the literacy gap before they enter kindergarten. A recent study by Hockenberger, Goldstein, and Haas (1999) demonstrated that simple changes in how mothers commented on storybooks with their preschool children resulted in improved emergent literacy skills in children who were at risk, as well as in children with developmental disabilities.

Equally important, the preschool years offer a critical opportunity to empower parents with the confidence and skills necessary to advocate for their children. By providing families positive experiences and relationships with educational personnel during the preschool years, teachers increase the likelihood that those parents will continue to have the courage to request partnerships with teachers as children struggle to achieve competence at school and in their home community.

❖ SUMMARY

Early childhood professionals have wonderful opportunities to help children from diverse backgrounds "beat the odds" as they enter formal schooling. Teachers can do much to prepare children for early school success by developing a strong commitment to creating a culturally responsive early childhood education program, by understanding the demands and expectations of formal literacy instruction the child will face in kindergarten and first grade, and by incorporating the kinds of strategies described here that support the development of emergent literacy in all children.

❖ REFERENCES

Adams, M. (1990). *Beginning to read: Thinking and learning about print*. Cambridge, MA: MIT Press.

Anderson, A. B., & Stokes, S. J. (1984). Social institutional influences on the development and practice of literacy. In H. Goelman, A. Oberg, & F. Smith (eds.), *Awakening to literacy*. Exeter, NH: Heinemann.

Au, K., & Kawakami, A. J. (1994). Cultural congruence in instruction. In E. R. Hollins, J. E. King, & W. C. Hayman (eds.), *Teaching diverse populations: Formulating a knowledge base* (p. 5–23). Albany: State University of New York Press.

Barrera, I. (1993). Effective and appropriate instruction for all children: The challenge of cultural/linguistic diversity and young children with special needs. *Topics in Early Childhood Special Education, 13*(4), 461–487.

Boykin, A. W. (1994). Afrocultural expression and its implications for schooling. In E. R. Hollins, J. E. King, & W. C. Hayman (eds.), *Teaching diverse populations: Formulating a knowledge base* (p. 243–274). Albany: State University of New York Press.

Chaney, C. (1990). Evaluating the whole language approach to language arts: The pros and cons. *Language, Speech and Hearing Services in the Schools, 21*(4), 244–249.

Clay, M. (1979). *Reading: The patterning of complex behaviour* (2nd ed.). Auckland, New Zealand: Heinemann Educational.

Clay, M. (1989). Concepts about print in English and other languages. *The Reading Teacher, 42*(4), 268–276.

Carrasco, R., Vera, A., & Cazden, C. B. (1981). Aspects of bilingual students' communicative competence: A case study. In R. P. Duran (ed.), *Latino language and communicative behavior*. Norwood, NJ: Ablex Publishers.

Cook-Gumperz, J., Gumperz, J., & Simons, H. (1981). School-Home ethnography project. (Final Report to the National Institute of Education). Washington, DC: U.S. Department of Education.

Cook, R. E., Tessier, A., & Klein, M. D. (2000). *Adapting early childhood curricula for children with special needs in inclusive setting* (5th ed.). Columbus, OH: Merrill/Prentice Hall.

Diaz, S., Moll, L. C., & Mehan, H. (1986). Sociocultural resources in instruction: A context specific approach. In
*Beyond language: Social and cultural factors in schooling
language minority students* (pp. 187–230). Los Angeles:
Evaluation Dissemination and Assessment Center, California State University.

Dickinson, D. K., DeTemple, J. M., Hirschler, J. A., & Smith,
M. W. (1992). Book reading with preschoolers: Co-
construction of text at home and at school. *Early Childhood Research Quarterly, 7,* 323–346.

Heath, S. B. (1986a). Taking a cross-cultural look at narratives. *Topics in Language Disorder, 7*(1), 84–96.

Heath, S. B. (1986b). Separating "things of the imagination"
from life: Learning to read and write. In W. H. Teale &
E. Sulzby (eds.), *Emergent literacy* (p.156–172). Norwood
NJ: Ablex Publishing.

Hildebrand, V. L., & Bader, L. A. (1992). An exploratory study
of parents' involvement in their child's emerging literacy skills. *Reading Improvement, 29,* 163–170.

Hockenberger, E. H., Goldstein, H., & Haas, L. S. (1999). Effects of commenting during joint book reading by
mothers with low SES. *Topics in Early Childhood Special
Education, 19*(1), 15–27.

Mason, J. M. (1992). Reading stories to children: A proposed
connection to reading. In P. Gough, L. Ehri, & R.
Treiman (eds.), *Reading Acquisition* (p. 215–242).
Hillsdale, NJ: Lawrence Erlbaum Associates.

McCormick, C. E., & Mason, J. M. (1986). Intervention procedures for increasing preschool children's interest in
and knowledge about reading. In W. H. Teale & E.
Sulzby (eds.), *Emergent literacy* (pp. 90–115). Norwood
NJ: Ablex Publishing.

Mehan, H. (1979). *Learning lessons: Social organization in the
classroom.* Cambridge, MA: Harvard University Press.

Morrison, G. S. (1991). *Early childhood education today* (5th
ed.). Columbus, Oh: Merrill.

National Research Council. (1998). *Preventing reading difficulties in young children.* Washington, DC: National Academy Press.

Neuman, S. B., & Roskos, K. (1994). Bridging home and
school with a culturally responsive approach. *Childhood
Education, 70*(4), 210–214.

Notari-Syverson, A., O'Connor, R. E., & Vadasy, P. F. (1998).
Ladders to literacy. A preschool activity book. Baltimore:
Paul H. Brookes Publishing.

Pewewardy, C. D. (1994). Culturally responsible pedagogy in
action: An American Indian magnet school. In E. R.
Hollins, J. E. King, & W. C. Hayman (eds.), *Teaching diverse populations: Formulating a knowledge base*
(p 77–92). Albany: State University of New York.

Phillips, C. B. (1994). The movement of African-American
children through sociocultural contexts. A case of conflict resolution. In B. L. Mallory & R. S. New (eds.),
Diversity and developmentally appropriate practices:

Challenges for early childhood education (p. 137–154). New York: Teachers College Press, Columbia University.

Reese, L., Balzano, S., Gallimore, R., & Goldenberg, G. (1991). The concept of Educacion: Latino family values and American schooling. Paper presented at the Annual Meeting of the American Anthropological Association.

Rush, K. L. (1999). Caregiver-child interactions and early literacy development of preschool children from low-income environments. *Topics in Early Childhood Special Education, 19*(1), 3–14.

Shade, B. J. (1994). Understanding the African-American learner. In E. R. Hollins, J. E. King, & W. C. Hayman (eds.), *Teaching diverse populations: Formulating a knowledge base* (p.175–190). Albany: State University of New York Press.

Snow, C. (1983). Literacy and language: Relationships during the preschool years. *Harvard Educational Review, 53*(2), 165–189.

Snow, C. (1993). Families as social contexts for literacy development. *New Directions for Child Development, 61,* 11–24.

Snow, C., Barnes, W. S., Chandler, J., Goodman, I. F. & Hemphill, L. (1991). *Unfulfilled expectations: Home and school influences on literacy.* Cambridge, MA: Harvard University Press.

Snow, C., & Ninio, A. (1986). The contracts of literacy: What children learn from learning to read books. In W. H. Teale & E. Sulzby (eds.), *Emergent literacy* (p. 116–138). Norwood, NJ: Ablex Publishing.

Sulzby, E. (1985). Children's emergent reading of favorite story books: A developmental study. *Reading Research Quarterly, 20*(4), 458–480.

Teale, W. H. (1986). Home background and young children's literacy development. In W. H. Teale & E. Sulzby (eds.), *Emergent literacy* (p. 173–206). Norwood NJ: Ablex Publishing.

Watson, L. R., Layton, T. L., Pierce, P. L., & Linzy, M. A. (1994). Enhancing emerging literacy in a language preschool. *Language, Speech and Hearing Services in Schools, 25*(3), 136–145.

Wells, G. (1982). Story reading and development of symbolic skills. *Australian Journal of Reading, 5,* 142–152.

Wells, G. (1985). Preschool literacy-related activities and success in school. In D. R. Olson, N. Torrance, & A. Hildyard (eds.), *Literacy, language and learning* (p. 229–255). New York: Cambridge University Press.

Williams, K. P. (1991). Storytelling as a bridge to literacy: An examination of personal storytelling among Black middle class mothers and children. *Journal of Negro Education, 60*(3), 399–410.

van Kleeck, A. (1990). Emergent literacy: Learning about print before learning to read. *Topics in Language Disorder, 10*(2), 25–45.

CHAPTER 7

Professional Development and Cultural Competence

The responsibility for supporting children from diverse backgrounds in early childhood settings is a very important one. As Saracho and Spodek (1995a) point out, the young child's socialization into the larger society should be an important goal of early childhood education. The transition from home to school is a difficult one for many children in the United States. They face a different language, different activities and materials, different expectations that relate to their interaction with adults, and different ways of using communication and interacting with peers. If we do not support these children through this crucial transition, their ability to successfully negotiate the next transition—to formal schooling—is seriously threatened.

Saracho & Spodek (1995b, p. 155) describe the professional attitudes and values that characterize early childhood professionals who work with children from linguistically and culturally diverse (LCD) backgrounds. These professionals:

- believe that cultural diversity is indeed a worthy goal;
- respect the culture children bring to school;
- believe that the children's culture is worth preserving and enriching;
- appreciate cultural and linguistic differences as undeniable individual differences;
- are willing to learn more about the education of LCD children;
- enhance children's self-image;
- have confidence in the ability of LCD children to learn; and
- have a positive attitude toward all children, regardless of social class.

Your professional development efforts to understand the needs of these children and to become truly culturally competent makes a significant difference in their lives. Your goal is to assist children and their families in understanding the dominant culture, and, at the same time, embrace and enhance their home culture. This chapter considers some key issues around the kind of professional development necessary to accomplish this.

❖ THE PROCESS OF PROFESSIONAL DEVELOPMENT

Professional development is a lifelong process that energizes our passion for our work and commitment to the field. The National Association for the Education of Young Children recommends 24 hours a year of professional development for early childhood professionals. Select professional development opportunities that build on your current role and experiences and provide practical strategies for your on-the-job needs. As you read this book, identify specific areas you would like to explore and learn more about. You may choose to use the *Early Childhood Professional Development Self-Assessment* in Appendix A at the end of this book to identify your strengths and needs in serving children and families from diverse cultural and linguistic backgrounds. High-quality and meaningful personal development takes time, planning, and commitment. Find a colleague whom you trust and respect and also is working on his or her own professional development. Team up for the process. Identify changes each of you would like to make in your own situations; and share observations, resources, and ideas for creating culturally responsive early childhood programs. Focus on making one change at a time, try out new ideas, evaluate what you tried, and share your experiments with your colleague.

Collegial support is an absolute necessity for personal development in early childhood education. Some programs build on opportunities for obtaining support through team-teaching situations, weekly staffings, or other planned activities. It is more enjoyable to team up with colleagues to attend courses, workshops, conferences, and other professional activities than attend them by yourself. Identify community activities and cultural events that increase your knowledge about, and understanding of, the families you serve. In addition, identify experienced professionals in the field of early childhood whom you trust and respect, have strong interpersonal skills and commitment to the profession, and have expertise working with families from diverse cultural and linguistic backgrounds. These persons could be colleagues in your program, professional acquaintances, or even your supervisor. Your relationship with a mentor may be formal or informal. Some early childhood programs assign mentors to new staff. Once you have identified a mentor, find time for regular communication, to share your concerns, and to listen.

Reflection, collaboration, and regularity are essential aspects of effective supervision and mentorship in work with young children and their families (Fenichel, 1992). Reflection involves the opportunity to step back from the immediate work experience and discuss experiences and concerns with a mentor. This is an opportunity to discuss cultural conflicts you experience with families. For example, how do you respond to a family's request to keep their daughter clean and tidy by restricting her play-based activities? It is important you acknowledge your own biases and understand there inevitably will be cultural conflicts that stem from differences between your program values and families' values.

Collaboration involves having "a friend on a difficult journey" to assist in navigating unfamiliar or challenging situations. It helps to have another person's perspective on difficult situations to identify possible options and resolutions. Having a trusted colleague with whom you discuss such dilemmas is important. Regular contact with your mentor is essential. It takes time and effort to develop a trusting relationship and a process for problem-solving. Clearly, administrative support is required to implement a formal mentorship process and to support its success in staff and program development, particularly in developing culturally responsive programs.

Ask yourself...

- *Does your job or certification require professional development goals?*
- *What are your professional development goals?*
- *What activities and resources should you use to achieve these goals?*
- *Who assists you in achieving your professional development goals?*
- *How did or can you identify a mentor and support for a relationship?*
- *What opportunities do you have to obtain collegial support?*
- *When did you draw on a colleague or mentor for support?*
- *When will you evaluate whether or not you have accomplished current goals or need to modify them, or add new ones?*

❖ PROGRAM DEVELOPMENT

Recently, the NAEYC took a strong position on the importance of understanding and using cultural context to inform practice in early childhood education (NAEYC, 1996; Bredekamp & Copple, 1997). This new position statement emphasizes that children's development is strongly influenced by the cultural context in which they live. Development Principle Number 6 states "Development and learning occur in and are influenced by multiple social and cultural contexts" (p. 12). As a result of their cultural context, children are taught, either explicitly or implicitly, specific behaviors such as how to show respect, how to interact with familiar and unfamiliar people, how to organize time and personal space, how to respond to transitions and celebrations, and so on.

This developmental principle is based on the 1996 NAEYC position statement on linguistic and cultural diversity. This position includes several clear statements of value around the design of culturally responsive early childhood programs.

**NAEYC Position Statement
on Linguistic and Cultural Diversity
(from NAEYC, 1996)**

• Recognize that all children are cognitively, linguistically, and emotionally connected to the language and culture of their home.
• Acknowledge that children can demonstrate their knowledge and capabilities in many ways.
• Understand that without comprehensible input, second-language learning can be difficult.
• Actively involve parents and families in the early learning program and setting.
• Encourage and assist all parents in becoming knowledgeable about the cognitive value for children of knowing more than one language, and provide them with strategies to support, maintain, and preserve home-language learning.
• Recognize that parents and families must rely on caregivers and educators to honor and support their children in the cultural values and norms of the home.
• Provide early childhood educators with professional preparation and development in the areas of culture, language and diversity.
• Recruit and support early childhood educators who are trained in languages other than English.
• Recognize that children can and will acquire the use of English even when their home-language is used and respected.
• Support and preserve home language usage.
• Develop and provide alternative and creative strategies for young children's learning.

Learning how to apply knowledge of culture in the early childhood setting is a complex and daunting task for teachers. It is also a lifelong process, one in which the more you know, the more complex it seems. The NAEYC (Bredekamp & Copple, 1997) recommends the first step, the one we described early in this text, is to

> "acknowledge that we are all influenced by cultural experiences and that just as children's development and learning is influenced by the context within which they live, teachers also are largely products of their experiences" (p. 42).

In addition to learning about one's own culture and developing a philosophy that values cultural diversity, there are many practical steps available to ensure that children's cultural backgrounds inform your day-to-day practice.

- Evaluate your program through a careful review of the materials, activities, and environment. Do you provide activities and use materials that teach about the diversity of everyone in your program, community, state, and country? This includes activities and materials that reflect diversity in gender and age; cultural, ethnic, and language backgrounds; work and occupations; and lifestyles (Jones & Derman-Sparks, 1992).
- Whenever possible, reflect the diversity of the children and families being served in the linguistic and ethnic make up of your program staff. Begin by identifying the cultural, ethnic, and linguistic make up of your program staff. One strategy is to recruit individuals from representative cultures to work in the program. Saracho and Spodek (1995b) recommend that early childhood professionals working with children from linguistically diverse backgrounds be fluent in two languages. However, given the rich cultural diversity of our country, a one-to-one match between staff and children's language background is not realistic. A program with five staff members can serve families from 15 different cultural backgrounds.

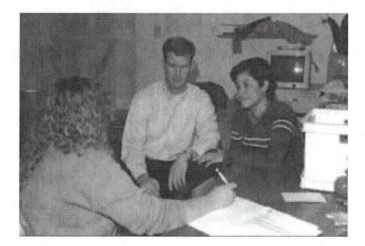

- Programs need to access bicultural/bilingual community resources.These include churches and other religious groups, business organizations, colleges and universities, and cultural clubs. Relationships with bicultural/bilingual individuals are a valuable asset to programs serving young children and families from diverse cultural backgrounds.
- Similar to the process of professional development, programs require ongoing review and modification to achieve and maintain quality services for young children and their families from diverse backgrounds. The Cultural competence self-assessment instrument (Child Welfare League of America, 1993), although not specifically for early childhood settings, provides a format for evaluating program services to culturally diverse children and families. There is an additional guide for self-assessment of cultural competencies in early childhood education, the *Early Childhood Professional Development: Self-Assessment in Cultural and Linguistic Diversity*, in Appendix A.
- At the program level, representative families should serve on advisory committees, participate in center activities, and serve as liaisons with the community; adapt the curriculum to reflect the context of the community; teachers should collaborate with each other in sharing resources and strategies for working with children from diverse backgrounds; and the program should build relationships with community groups (Ramsey & Derman-Sparks, 1992). For example, the program should work with community groups of diverse cultures to ensure materials are authentic versus stereotypical and reflect the culture. What are true representations of Native American dress? Representatives from the community can serve as liaisons between the program and families to build a partnership between home and center.
- Develop more than just a local knowledge of the cultures represented in your program. A broader understanding of the history, heroes, and symbols of the culture, as well as what is considered aesthetic and artful in a culture's music, dance, art, and literature, is not only important but also

enjoyable. For example, United States history books often do not include detailed or accurate portrayals of the historical roles and contributions of minority groups. It takes some effort to gain this knowledge.

Ask yourself . . .

- *What resources does your program have to serve children and families from diverse cultures? Does staff reflect the cultural and linguistic diversity of families in the program? Does your staff include trained interpreters?*
- *Who is represented on your program advisory and decision-making committees? Do representatives reflect the cultural and linguistic diversity of the children and families in your program?*
- *What organizations are accessible in the community that represent various cultural, ethnic, and language groups? Are there religious, social service, or business groups that serve a particular cultural or linguistic group in the community?*
- *What is the program mechanism for family/professional collaboration regarding curriculum development and instructional practices? Is there a committee process for identifying family and program concerns and priorities, for gathering input from families and staff, and for recommending program practices?*
- *How does your program evaluate its effectiveness in serving children and families from diverse backgrounds? Is there an annual evaluation process involving a family questionnaire or interview? How are results shared and used to modify or determine program goals for the future?*

❖ RELATIONSHIP OF CULTURALLY RESPONSIVE PRACTICES TO ETHICAL CONDUCT

The NAEYC has produced an extensive Code of Ethical Conduct (NAEYC, 1997). This document recognizes that ethical dilemmas will always exist and that often the "right answer" to such dilemmas is not immediately obvious. Several guidelines lie within this code that relate specifically to cultural issues.Two of the "core values" stated as the basis for the Code of Ethical Conduct are:

1. A commitment to appreciating and supporting the close ties between the child and family.
2. Recognizing that children are best understood and supported in the context of family, culture, community, and society.

In addition, the Code includes several principles that address cultural issues:

P-1.2: We shall not participate in practices that discriminate against children by denying benefits, giving special advantages, or excluding them from programs or activities on the basis of their race, ethnicity, religion, sex, national origin, language, ability, or the status, behavior, or beliefs of their parents. (This principle does not apply to programs that have a lawful mandate to provide services to a particular population of children.)

1-2.3: To respect the dignity of each family and its culture, language, customs, and beliefs.

1-2.4: To respect families' childrearing values and their right to make decisions for their children.

When ethical dilemmas occur that involve cultural issues, we recommend that the practitioner, together with a supervisor or mentor, apply "third space" thinking, as described by Brown and Barrera (1999). Third space thinking moves away from an effort to determine what is "right" by way of a dichotomous, binary way of thinking ("this culture versus that culture" or "my way or your way"), and moves toward a sort of "holographic" view in which we see both sides at once (the "third space"). This allows for the creation of new patterns and ways of understanding.

❖ SUMMARY

We do not pretend that this process is an easy one. Good intentions are necessary but not sufficient for the successful development of truly culturally responsive and developmentally appropriate and enhancing early childhood programs.

Professional and program development is a systematic, dynamic, and ongoing process. As a new professional, you will focus on developing competent skills in particular job-related responsibilities, and on promoting your identity as an early childhood professional. As an experienced professional, you will hone your skills, identity new goals for professional development, and perhaps mentor a new professional.

Your have chosen to contribute to a significant profession that makes a difference in the lives of your children. As an early childhood professional, you have the role, responsibility, and opportunity—in partnership with families—to guide young children during an exciting journey of discovery and accomplishment. Each child brings his or her cultural and family background, abilities, temperament, and other qualities to the program. As an early childhood professional, you have the responsibility to craft an environment that is developmentally appropriate and supports the development of skills that facilitate the child's participation in the larger community and in later life. All young children need a sense of cultural identity, of their family heritage, and of the larger community. Your role is to create a balance in the learning environment that will support the children's entrance to the larger community by respecting what they bring with them, appreciating the differences, building on similarities, and celebrating the riches of diversity.

❖ REFERENCES

Bredekamp, S., & Copple, C. (eds.). (1997). *Developmentally Appropriate Practice in Early Childhood Programs* (rev. ed.). Washington, DC: National Association for the Education of Young Children.

Brown, W., & Barrera, I. (1999). Enduring problems in assessment: The persistent challenges of cultural dynamics and family issues. *Infants and Young Children, 12*(1), 34–42.

Child Welfare League of America. (1993). *Cultural competence self-assessment instrument.* Washington, DC: Author.

Fenichel, E. (1992). *Learning through supervision and mentorship.* Arlington, VA: Zero to Three/National Center for Clinical Infant Programs.

Jones, E., & Derman-Sparks, L. (1992). Meeting the challenge of diversity. *Young Children, 47*(2), 12–18.

National Academy of Early Childhood Programs. (1984). Accreditation criteria and procedures of the National

Academy of Early Childhood Programs. Washington, DC: National Association for the Education of Young Children.

National Association for the Education of Young Children. (1991). Accreditation criteria and procedures of the National Academy of Early Childhood Programs (rev. ed.). Washington, DC: National Association for the Education of Young Children.

NAEYC. (1996). NAEYC Position Statement: Responding to linguistic and cultural diversity. Recommendations for effective early childhood education. *Young Children, 51*(4), 4–12.

National Association for the Education of Young Children. (1997b). Code of ethical conduct. http:// www. naeyc. org.

Ramsey, P. G., & Derman-Sparks, L. (1992). Multicultural education reaffirmed. *Young Children, 47*(2), 10–11.

Saracho, O. N., & Spodek, B. (1995a). The future challenge of linguistic and cultural diversity in the schools. In E. Garcia & B. McLaughlin (eds.), *Meeting the challenge of linguistic and cultural diversity in early childhood education* (pp. 170–173). New York: Teachers College Press.

Saracho, O. N., & Spodek, B. (1995b). Preparing teachers for early childhood programs of linguistic and cultural diversity. In E. Garcia & B. McLaughlin (eds.), *Meeting the challenge of linguistic and cultural diversity in early childhood education* (pp. 154–169). New York: Teachers College Press.

❖ APPENDIX A

Early Childhood Professional Development: Self-Assessment in Cultural and Linguistic Diversity

Name _____ Date _____

Position _____ Program _____

Please rate yourself on your knowledge and ability in the following areas:

I. Self-Awareness	**Low**			**High**
A. Understands:				
1. Cultural influences on own values and behaviors.	1	2	3	4
2. Own biases related to child-rearing and family roles.	1	2	3	4
3. How own biases conflict with others.	1	2	3	4
B. Has the ability to:				
1. Recognize when biases interfere with own attitudes and relationships with family or child.	1	2	3	4
2. Use strategies to reduce effects of own bias.	1	2	3	4
3. Value and enhance child's culture when different from own.	1	2	3	4

II. Families	**Low**			**High**
A. Understands:				
1. Cultural factors that influence families' expectation of early childhood programs.	1	2	3	4
2. Cultural influences on family's child-rearing practices.	1	2	3	4
3. Cultural and family communication style influences on language development.	1	2	3	4
4. Cultural influences in family's attitudes toward and interactions with professionals.	1	2	3	4

B. Has the ability to:

1. Accept family differences and use these characteristics as strengths in the instructional process.   1   2   3   4

2. Communicate effectively with individuals from a range of different cultures.   1   2   3   4

3. Communicate in culturally appropriate ways about the program's philosophy, goals, and expectations.   1   2   3   4

4. Assist families in their understanding about attitudes, lifestyles, and educational practices in the United States.   1   2   3   4

III. Cultural Influences on Child Behavior   **Low**   **High**

A. Understands influence of culture on development:

1. Communication skills and styles.   1   2   3   4

2. Social and play skills and behaviors.   1   2   3   4

3. Child-adult interaction.   1   2   3   4

B. Understands the influence of culture on emergent literacy and development of preacademic skills

1. Can identify a wide range of culturally valid ways to help support emergent literacy.   1   2   3   4

2. Supports the development of preacademic skills in ways that are culturally relevant and meaningful.   1   2   3   4

C. Has the ability to:

1. Create a nurturing and secure environment that respects cultural differences and accommodates child's individual needs.   1   2   3   4

2. Utilize relevant information and instructional strategies and materials in learning activities.   1   2   3   4

3. Utilize learning activities
and instructional strategies
that reduce bias and racism
in young children.   1   2   3   4

IV. Assessment   **Low**   **High**
A. Understands:
  1. Issues and problems
    associated with use of
    standardized assessment of
    culturally or linguistically
    different children.   1   2   3   4
  2. Nonbiased ecologically
    valid assessment procedures
    and techniques.   1   2   3   4
  3. Importance of determining
    cultural norms for child
    behavior and development. 1   2   3   4
B. Has the ability to:
  1. Conduct appropriate
    nonbiased assessment of
    infants and young children. 1   2   3   4
  2. Generate developmentally
    appropriate goals and
    practices related to assessment
    result and family priorities. 1   2   3   4

**V. Bilingual Language
Development**   **Low**   **High**
A. Understands:
  1. Similarities in process of
    first and second language
    acquisition.   1   2   3   4
  2. Importance of strengthening/
    maintaining child's primary
    language and facilitating
    family-child
    communication.   1   2   3   4
  3. Cultural influences on
    children's nonverbal
    communicative behavior.   1   2   3   4
  4. Ways in which home
    culture influences
    communication styles in
    the classroom.   1   2   3   4

B. Has the ability to:

	Low			High
1. Facilitate acquisition of English as a second language.	1	2	3	4
2. Facilitate and/or maintain the child's first language.	1	2	3	4
3. Facilitate those language skills that directly influence academic readiness and early literacy.	1	2	3	4
4. Facilitate pragmatic communication skills that enhance children's social skills.	1	2	3	4

VI. Use of Interpreters

	Low			High
A. Understands:				
1. Appropriate and ethical use of interpreters.	1	2	3	4
2. Guidelines related to strategies and techniques of effective interpretation.	1	2	3	4
B. Has the ability to:				
1. Interpret for families and service providers.	1	2	3	4
2. Select and use an interpreter appropriately.	1	2	3	4

VII. Evaluation Summary

Low   **High**

A. Professional Development

1. What are your areas of strength when working with children and families from diverse cultural and linguistic backgrounds?

2. What areas need development to work more effectively with children and families from diverse cultural and linguistic backgrounds?

B. Program Development
    1. To what degree does your
       program meet the needs of
       children and families from
       diverse cultural and linguistic
       backgrounds?   1   2   3   4

2. What do you see as your program's strengths in working with families and young children from diverse cultural and linguistic backgrounds?

3. What areas does your program need to develop in servicing a diverse population more effectively?

Index

Aboud, F., 123
Academic skills, 48. *See also* School
  achievement
  value placed on, 86, 114
Accommodations for religious practices, 11-12
Accounts, 141. *See also* Narratives
Accreditation, 31
Acculturation, 4-5, 8
  degree of, 22, 76, 89
  to formal schooling, 189
  Latino families, 91
  rejection of home culture during,
  23
Achievement pressure, 80
Activities, 9. *See also* Play
  affirming culture/ethnicity in,
  128-30, 189
  for language development and
  acquisition, 159
  level of, 117
  messy, 118, 120
  physically oriented, 188
  unfamiliar, 47, 117
Adaptation to physical environment, 6
Adler, S., 109
Adult-child interaction, 44, 104,
  105-11. *See also* Communication
  African American children, 106-7
  Asian American children, 107-8,
  139
  child-initiated, 172
  children's degree of comfort in,
  111
  conversational, 107, 139
  educator-child, 118, 128-30, 188
  effect on communication skills,
  134
  formal, 107
  initiation of, 105-6, 172
  intermediaries for, 108, 139
  for language development, 152
  in Native American cultures, 96
  nonverbal communication in,
  116
  triadic, 139
  verbal, 144
Adulthood, preparation for, 96
Adults. *See also* Parents; Teachers
  children's interactions with. *See*
  Adult-child interaction
  respect for, 108
Affiliation, 89, 96, 108
  group, 124
  time of, 126

African Americans, 62-64. *See also*
  Racism
  child-rearing practices, 81-89, 106
  gender roles and, 117-18
  overindulgence and, 72-73
  parents' teaching role, 73-74
  view of physical development, 80
Age, 5, 13, 18-19
Age appropriateness, 31
Aggressiveness, 7
  expression of, 123
  in verbal interactions, 106, 138
Altruism, 109, 111, 112
Ambition, 12
Ancestors, 86, 87
Anderson, A. B., 181, 182, 183, 184
Anderson, P., 95
Anti-Bias Curriculum (Derman-
  Sparks), 117, 126
Asian cultures, 15
  child-rearing practices, 85-89
  family roles in, 70-71
  filial piety in, 70
  gender roles and, 118
  immigrants from, 2
  independence in, 73
  interdependence as value, 114
  parent-child interaction in, 75
  storytelling, 142
  subgroups of, 85
  teaching in, 74
Asian families, traditional, 85-89,
  110, 139
Assertiveness, 80, 81
  verbal, 110, 171
Assimilation, 4
Au, K., 188
Authority, 87
  challenging, 16, 71
  deference to, 15-16, 87, 89, 107
  of father, 92
Autonomy, 46, 110
  early, 111
  value placed on, 61, 95

Backchanneling, 107
Bader, L. A., 181
Barrera, I., 188, 189, 204
Basic interpersonal communication
  skill (BICS), 148
Baumrind, D., 83
Behavior
  aggressive, 7
  appropriate, 48. *See also* proper,
  this heading

BEHAVIOR (*continued*)
bad, 111
changes in, 111
communicative value of, 73
conventional, 37
cultural differences' influence
on, 3
effects on others, 114
expectations for, 135
families' expectations re, 43,
71, 89
home/school conflicts, 28, 189
play, 104. *See also* Play
proper, 86, 89, 92
respectful, 169
rules for, 107-8, 116
shared patterns, 4
social, 5, 75
socioeconomic status and, 17
teaching, 199
verbal, 71-72, 138-39
Beizer, L., 64
Belief systems, 4, 122. *See also* Values
Biases, 40, 130. *See also* Prejudice;
Stereotypes; Values
BICS (basic interpersonal communi-
cation skill), 148
Biculturalism, 23, 168
Bidialecticalism, 152
Bien educada, 91, 109
Bigler, R. A., 122
Bilingual education, 19-20, 35
Bilingualism, 147
Birthright, 13
Black English Dialect, 151
Body language, 8. *See also*
Communication, nonverbal
Bornstein, M. H., 88
Boykin, W., 63
Briggs, C. L., 72
Brown, Roger, 138
Brown, W., 204
Bruner, J., 74
Buddhism, 85

Call and response activities, 159
CALP (cognitive academic language
proficiency), 149, 150
Cambodian culture, 88
Caregivers
grandmothers/aunts, 93
multiple, 82
non-family members as, 69, 70
siblings as, 70
Caregiving, 48
inconsistent, 60, 82
by non-family members, 69, 70
Carrasco, R., 188
Categorization, 121, 122, 127
Cazden, C. B., 188

Central America, 2
Ceremony, 94, 95
Chan, S., 87, 88
Chaney, C., 176
Cheng, L. L., 108
Cheng, L. R., 146, 160
Child-rearing practices
African Americans, 81-89
basis of, 58
for children with disabilities, 21
consistency in, 70
factors affecting, 58
group characteristics, 76, 81
judgments re, 62
Latino cultures, 89-93
mainstream culture match, 135
mainstream middle-class, 59,
76-81, 97-98
Native American cultures, 93-97
non-family members' role, 93
reliance on experts, 74
religion and, 18
respecting, 204
stress and, 60-61
variances in, 3, 43-45, 48, 76, 97
Children
affective connection to mother,
115
contextual understanding of,
199, 204
expectations for, 43-45, 46
interests of, 31-32
learning from culture, 5
in poverty, 11
responsibilities of, 81, 89
ties to family, 204
Chinese Americans, 108
Chinn, Philip C., 3
Chipman, M., 124
Choices, 119
Class, social. *See* Social class
Classification. *See* Categorization
Code-switching, 152
Cognitive academic language proficiency (CALP), 149, 150
Cognitive development, 120-26. *See
also* Learning
Cognitive style, 85
Collaboration, 168, 198
Communication. *See also* Language
adult-child, 71-72, 73, 84, 87-88.
See also Adult-child interaction
child-initiated, 141, 144
in classroom, 152-63
cultural differences' influence
on, 3
describing the obvious, 140-41,
144-45, 172
familiar methods of, 173
"high context" cultures, 8, 13, 84, 92